FEAR,
TRUTH,
WRITING

THE SUNY SERIES IN
POSTMODERN CULTURE
Joseph Natoli, Editor

FEAR, TRUTH, WRITING

From Paper Village
to Electronic Community

Alison Leigh Brown

State University of New York Press

808.02
B877f

Published by
State University of New York Press, Albany

© 1995 State University of New York

All rights reserved

Printed in the United States of America

For information, address State University of New York
Press, State University Plaza, Albany, N.Y., 12246

Production by Diane Ganeles
Marketing by Nancy Farrell

Library of Congress Cataloging-in-Publication Data

Brown, Alison Leigh, 1959–
    Fear, truth, writing : from paper village to electronic
community/ Alison Leigh Brown.
        p.   cm. — (SUNY series, postmodern culture)
    Includes bibliographical references.
    ISBN 0-7914-2532-0 (pbk. : alk. paper). — ISBN 0-7914-2531-2
(CH : alk. paper)
    1. Authorship.   2. Authorship—Data processing.   3. Fear in
literature.   4. Truth in literature.   I. Title.   II. Series: SUNY
series in postmodern culture.
PN51.B795 1995
808′.02—dc20
                                                            94-32800
                                                            CIP

10 9 8 7 6 5 4 3 2 1

CONTENTS

PREFACE

I was motivated to write this book because of two pressing concerns. The first has to do with the increasingly blurry
boundaries amongst different kinds of writing: fiction, theory, critical theory, and "straight" academese. The second
reason has to do with a feeling of anxiety surrounding the
role of the college or university in the production, dissem-
ination, and erasing of "culture."

My first concern was easy to work out. I simply wrote as
I needed to write in order to underline the lack of boundaries
between these kind of writings. I don't think that it is embarrassing to say that sometimes it was embarrassing to write
the book as it is written. I felt as if I were spying on myself.
More seriously, I increasingly feel as if certain sorts of connections need to be exploited for us to understand what we
mean by interdisciplinary work—something so many of us
find exciting and necessary. To break down the walls of the
disciplines, we need to do more than talk to our colleagues in
other disciplines—although this is a very good start. We
must, to allude to Cixous, break down our own walls.

"Colleagues" above refers to other college or university
professors. I hope, and I believe, that breaking down academic boundaries is of importance outside of academe. One
of the theses of this book is that social action is sometimes
curtailed because of a fear of acquiring knowledge about
ourselves. We become different through action, writing, discussion. Certain sorts of changes do not allow us to revert to
our old ways and we mostly know and understand the
significance of that. It can feel better, then, to give into our
fear and act out positions that lead to serial repetition and

not to change. But this posture is devastating to us both personally and socially. I write here about an easy way of overcoming fear: writing to ourselves about ourselves. I still believe that changes in consciousness are crucial ones—ones that have broad social impact. Writing is better than *merely* thinking because it leaves a trace. Thoughts are more easily repressed. Writing has to be physically destroyed, nevertheless it leaves traces.

My second concern is much more difficult. Academic institutions and the persons who run them, work for them, and study at them are clearly anxious. The anxiety is allowed to focus, for instance, on budgetary concerns, or on the dismal job market of the "real world," but an underlying locus is less scrutinized. This is not to say, to be sure, that no scrutiny exists. There is plenty of hand-wringing about our role(s). But the root radical questions are not discussed as often as they should be. Is it possible to be postmodernist from a modern institution? Is it possible to meaningfully discuss social change from institutions that still echo century old hierarchies? (I can hear a reader snort: "Echo?! How about *scream*?) How far do we want to dismantle those hierarchies? If each text we study erases its others *in that moment*, how do we decide which lesson to teach? How can we change the ways that texts are chosen? To what extent do we want to change them? Can we teach deconstruction before we teach . . . well, what? How long can we read and write about margins and marginal voices from our positions of safety without beginning to disrespect ourselves? But how can we fail to read and write about margins and marginal voices? How much of the institution do we coddle in order to have the freedom to change those things that need changing? Can we have integrity if we work in an institution that shares none or few of our educational, ethical, or political goals? I wonder almost simultaneously how to reconcile the mammoth contradictions that confront us and how to contain my pleasure at being alive when so much magnificent work is being produced. Can we shake the need, the desire, for reconciliation and closure? This concern, this anxiety, is only skated over here.

ACKNOWLEDGMENTS

For helping me maintain community and (mostly) sanity I thank my colleagues at Northern Arizona University. Susan Foster-Cohen, in particular, gave good advice and friendship. For reading and commenting on portions of this text I thank Joe Boles, Steven Harvey, and David Mertz. Andrew Cutrofello has long been a reliable and helpful reader—I'm grateful to him. Bill Martin and Kelly Oliver were careful readers. The Sedona sisters kept me laughing. Riley Speckart proves continuity.

Thanks to J. Dette Avalon for helping me focus "other" creative energies; Sheila Brown for teaching me that the only undeniable value was truth; Barbara Harvey for being a fearless feminist; Jennifer Harvey for being fierce and brave; Sara Jensen for being so beautiful with Amanda that I had to have Zoe; Elizabeth Segars for loving me when unlovable and giving me something to work for; Becky Thomas for making me remember community even when I didn't want to, and, of course, Tamsin Lorraine for giving me a richer and more significant understanding of both family and community.

I have been lucky to have good teachers. I am indebted especially to Bob Ackermann, but also to Ann Ferguson, Fred Hagen, and Tom Reed.

An organized research grant from Northern Arizona University (Summer 1993) facilitated the writing of this book. I am grateful for it.

For kindly granting me permission to reprint from their publications, thanks to the following publishers:

From *Phenomenology of Spirit* by G.W.F. Hegel, translated by A.V. Miller, copyright 1977 by Oxford University Press, by permission of Oxford University Press.

From "Free Your Mind and Your Ass Will Follow," on *Free Your Mind and Your Ass Will Follow*, Funkadelic, copyright 1989 Westbound Records, Bridgeport Music (BMI)— used by permission.

From *In Memoriam to Identity* by Kathy Acker. Copyright 1990 by Grove/Atlantic, Inc., by permission of Grove/Atlantic, Inc.

From the essays "But Beyond . . ." by Jacques Derrida, translated by Peggy Kamuf, *Critical Inquiry*, 13; and, "Like the Sound of the Sea Deep Within the Shell," by Jacques Derrida, translated by Peggy Kamuf, *Critical Inquiry*, 14, used by permission of W.J.T. Mitchell.

INTRODUCTION

> Before being so radically and purposely the ges-
> ture of Heidegger, this gesture was also made by
> Nietzsche and Freud, both of whom, as is well known,
> and sometimes in very similar fashion, put conscious-
> ness into question in its assured certainty of itself.[1]

1. Truth, Fear, and Writing

Spinoza of course made this gesture before it could have
been made.[2] Consciousness can no longer be certain of itself;
and if it cannot now, then it never could have been. The
difference between then and now, is that self-doubt is self-
conscious at every level. Our obsessions here find their way
into journals, letter-writing, e-mail communities, writing of
all sorts.[3] So much of what we write about in each case, is
why we are writing. As "authors" become increasingly self-
conscious about what they are doing, that is, as they become
increasingly aware that they are writing and re-writing
themselves in an effort to keep themselves in existence,[4]
philosophical writing increasingly chooses as its subject its
own process.[5] In my title I have juxtaposed writing with fear
and with truth. The gesture toward fear must seem just a
little odd; that toward truth, perhaps even quaint. My point
is that we write because we are afraid of truth: sometimes

we write to overcome that fear, and in overcoming that fear we find something other than fear; other times we write to cover up the fear by obscuring the truth.[6]

There are two reasons I find the study of these relations important. First, I believe that the primary impediment to organized political action (revolution) is fear. We are afraid to form the requisite communities for political action because of brute counter force, of course, also, and importantly, because of the fear of discovering ourselves in this or that configuration. Who will we be? What will we become?[7] Second, I will argue that writing, text-making of all kinds, is the foundation of communities. We commune with those whose writing touches us, or is capable of touching us. As such every graphematic structure is endlessly important as signifier and signified.

So fear and writing have significant consequences. Why truth? It is so . . . old fashioned. Truth, in my view, configures every action, each gesture, it is the sum of each stroke of the pen, each tap of the keyboard, indeed, each surreptitious glance in the mirror. Who will I be when I catch myself? Who will we be when we pause? Truth is not some quality attached either to words and their relations to objects, nor some property inherent in some state of affair, nor yet some coherence of theories making a web over our dusty universe. Instead, truth just is. If there is, and there is, then it is true. Every bit of it. An illusion is as true as a dream; my love is as true as my hate.

Connections between truth, fear, and writing are there (consciously and unconsciously). The connections are crucially important, for if we recognize them and use them, our writing will be better and we will be better. This is a book about writing to better ourselves. Another way to put this is that it is a book that offers one practical suggestion with respect to coming to understand ourselves. The practical suggestion is that when we write we should try to abandon ourselves to the point that we overcome our fear. We can do this by realizing that we need not save our writing, we need not share it, we need not re-read it. We may decide that we want to do all of these things. Let this, the level of sorting, be our level of fear.

When we write ourselves, we are forced to think about all of our possibilities. We can cover over this or we can face it. In either case writing is a specific case of becoming _____, where _____ is what we need or desire for ourselves or our communities. Writing is one of the few practices that is necessarily emancipatory.[8]

As you might imagine these words, those you are reading now, are written after the fact of the other (real) writing—that which produced the books. When the major words, those which make up the actual studies, were written, it was not with the conscious aim in mind to analyze why we write. But this is what they have done. I started out to find the underlying ethics in the writers I either admire or feel I should admire; I ended up finding a method for writing ourselves, or even more precisely, the selves that we are *not*. However, when this is baldly explicit, the experience acquired is intensified but the ability to share the writing will diminish for many. Privacy issues come up here.[9]

In philosophy, privacy has been closely guarded. "I am not speaking for myself but of the general man. Later, I will not be speaking for myself but of the general woman. Later still, I will not be speaking for myself but of the general possibility of multiple selves." This hiding of the author belies a justified paranoia. If our philosophical thoughts are just claimed, we will be thought of as insane. Only a philosopher could write in all seriousness: 'I act with *complete* certainty. But this certainty is my own,'(Wittgenstein 1972, paragraph 174). Only a philosopher could make this "I" every "I" and hence lend credibility to the "utterance." The fear behind such an assertion is palpable. The content of this paragraph has been chosen; it has not been thrown out. It bore saying and writing. What if that paragraph were not attached to Wittgenstein *qua* philosopher? What if a lesser philosopher mouths those words? A salesperson? A lunatic? A drag queen? A führer?

Foucault has already played with these themes in his

writing, but then he does something strange: he allows himself to be interviewed on condition that he not be named. He becomes the masked philosopher *saying* not *writing* things like: "I would say at this point that philosophy is a way of reflecting on our relation to the truth. But it must not end there. It's a way of asking oneself: if such is the relation that we have with truth, then how should we conduct ourselves?" (Foucault 198,, 201). Philosophy's task could not have been done without the mask. It would sound, and be, ridiculous, naive. Because philosophers mean these things, they expose their fear. Fear motivates claims of subjective truth and, in turn, the claims cover up fear. Uncovering the being of fear involves using fear up. If absence of fear can lead to empowerment, then writing is necessary to that process.

Assume that making texts, writing words, turns out always to be political. Now notice Aristotle saying:

> with regard to the things that are done from fear of greater evils or for some noble object (e.g. if a tyrant were to order one to do something base, having one's parents and children in his power, and if one did the action they were to be saved, but otherwise would be put to death), it may be debated whether such actions are involuntary or voluntary (Aristotle 1941, III,I,1110).

Is it the fear that calls into question the moral responsibility for the base deed in this case? Or is it fear that forces us to make meaning both in the linguistic and moral spheres of our lives? Aristotle viewed fear as neither virtue nor vice. Instead context and object determined when fear is good, when bad. Fear of the wrong things is the root of cowardice; fear of the right things an indication of wisdom, even of bravery.

The text from Aristotle helps us see that it is possible to do the right thing even though motivated by fear. But fear, as a subjective state of mind, is therefore not sufficient for producing the right thing. Fear is neutral in general; with specificity, it becomes a category for analysis (not of analysis). This state of mind that Aristotle describes, is one where the state of mind itself cannot let us determine whether something is "right." Context and object are necessary for this determination. The subjective state is what can never be denied; its expression, however, cannot be certain of itself: hence the need to write and re-write. Nietzsche says:

> We no longer esteem ourselves sufficiently when we communicate ourselves. Our true experiences are not at all garrulous. They could not communicate themselves even if they tried. That is because they lack the right word. Whatever we have words for, that we have already got beyond. In all talk there is a grain of contempt. Language, it seems, was invented only for what is average, medium, communicable. With language the speaker immediately vulgarizes himself. Out of a morality for deaf-mutes and other philosophers (Nietzsche 1954, pp. 530–31).

Nietzsche, like Heidegger, senses a tension between language and an experience which lies beneath it. But part of what they are each looking for is Heidegger himself, Nietzsche himself. Derrida presents Nietzsche as one who has a duty to say *who he is*, and also as one who knows that the answer (to "who am I?") is not an identity. Nietzsche says that "he has seen the dawning of a 'hidden history' of philosophers—*he does not say of philosophy*—and the 'psychology of their great names'" (Derrida 1988, p. 24).

Hegel doesn't sign—the system goes on without him. Nietzsche wants to sign. "It appears that Nietzsche signs and signs more than once. He is someone who writes his autobiography, recalls his name, his genealogy, and so forth" (Derrida 1988, p. 56). But in fact Hegel signs by not signing and does so with less trouble than does Nietzsche. When we write, we write also for the dead. Lately, some of the emphasis on the writing of dead people has been, "were they fascists?" This question puzzles me. If it is so important (and it is) why is it reserved for the dead. More importantly, why is it reserved for others? We need to ask ourselves at least as often as we ask of others: "What of my writing, what of my reading denies fascism?" and "What of my text making and re-making assents to fascism?" I talk about signing my name to writing and thereby remind myself and my readers that I insert myself, in part, into this analysis as an object of analysis. And in fearing, fear can then look at the fearsome explicitly, and 'make it clear' to itself" (Heidegger 1962, p. 180). Part of what fear makes clear to itself is that the subjective status of one "I" is not universal.[10] "That which fear fears about is that very entity which is afraid—Dasein. Only an entity for which in its Being this very being is an issue, can be afraid. Fearing discloses this entity as endangered and abandoned to itself" (Heidegger 1962, p. 181). My question, then, is not what *is* this person, this author? I believe that question to be irrelevant. My questions always concern "What I am becoming through the textual process?" "What are the communities made possible through such processes?" and "Which of these communities aid and abet revolution?" I would change "biography" to "zoography" or better still to "zoographical implication analysis."

2. When Writing is Not

If there were something like absolute silence, it would be very fear-inducing. Silence, means the absence of sound, of context. We rush in to fill emptiness with sound in what seems a natural way. We speak, but this is too ethereal. We write but this is too private. So, we write-for-a-public but the more conscious we are of why we write the less we want to claim the writing as our own. So what is it that we fear when we read and write? The answer has to be determined, in part, through the strange language and paradigms we have traditionally used for truth. We might conclude that we must free ourselves for truth in Heidegger's narrowest sense. We need to see texts as the evolutionary things that they are: they are determined, in part, by other texts, by those who read them. Freeing ourselves to this reality need not affect what is scientific about what we do. It will serve to remind us of the objective in the subjective and the subjective in the objective. "Men have judged that a king can make rain; *we* say this contradicts all experience. Today they judge that aeroplanes and the radio, etc., are means for the closer contact of peoples and the spread of culture" (Wittgenstein 1972, paragraph 132). There are reasons not to so conclude. If we free ourselves for truth, then something of the responsibility or choice with respect to our commitments seems to vanish. Heidegger seems to deny the *sense* of such talk. Wittgenstein relegates us to games and rules with responsibility reserved for mystics.

For strategic purposes, Derrida finds it necessary to recast the concept of text as encompassing everything. This sidesteps the need to free ourselves, to open ourselves for meaning. But how are his readers to act in face of all-enveloping texts?[11] And in fact, few writers have introduced more novelty of form than Derrida himself. We have the suggestive pin-ups,[12] the off-size texts, the marginal wanderings, the strike-outs and so on. But what about giving up the structure? How about letting beings be? When we write about situations requiring action, or talk about them, the discourse should match the temporal exigencies involved. Can there be a fruitful dialectic between letting things be and trying to master contexts?

This is a book, in the end, about politics. Political writing has been too careful. One must be wary of letting beings be in one specific way. Namely, one ought not interpret the letting be as an absolution of one's responsibility in the world one constitutes and that one is constituted by. Still, it is frightening to write because it may turn out that we are the "they." That we are no better than Heidegger who writes to us about the "they" but who is one of "them" is the frightening possibility that we must not repress. We are afraid of writing because it is (potentially) public analysis. Philosophical and psychoanalytical analysis may differ only with respect to venue. We must overcome this fear by recognizing it and not succumbing to it in order to hide it.

I am trying to articulate the fear that motivates and paralyzes. This double edged movement that lets us pretend that we are notions and that denies that we are. The fear that is more comfortably directed at those who are no longer among us, as if problems of oppression, problems of fascism are a distant fear, a nightmare, not a reality. What is written must first be thought. What is thought is uncovered in/by/through our previous and future thinking. We cover our thinking, in part, because of fear. Fear blocks writing. Fear blocks truth. Fear blocks truth and writing by covering truth and writing. The initial covering of things relates to our fear of them. The uncovering in writing and speech is an overcoming of fear. This is the direction in which we are going although we have not yet specified what kind of relation exists between fear and writing, fear and the entities covered. The exact relationship is not one I can generalize. If "I" could generalize, "I" would be a situationist. If "I" could generalize, "I" could find an argument for anarcho-syndicalism, for example.

3. *Thought Speaking then Writing Itself*

Sometimes universal statements help us understand particular things in the world. The lesson from Kojeve's Hegel is that most pertinent to speech and writing is that the freedom to be "I" entails the beginning of time as the end of history. This should paralyze us. Kojeve's Hegel is a terrifying vision. If it were once capable of being instantiated it would already be instantiated and we would all be silent. Because we speak and because sometimes we even speak as other than ourselves (in the sense of I = I, the I equal to itself), that vision is not possibly "true." What is important to this discussion is that there is never a speaking "I" equal to "it's" "self." Processses which hide thought thereby minimizing writing. Television hides thought. Education hides thought. Sexism hides thought. Classism hides thought. Racism hides thought. But importantly, each of these ism's mimic thought in exacting detail. As automata, we parrot again and again the script that we are denying.

4. *Writing Ourselves*

That Are Not. I can write about three distinct experiences one might have while writing. I could write about more than three. I could spend the rest of my life writing about the distinct experiences one might have while writing. Some writing experiences could never be written but I could gesture toward those. I could make this my life's work. One distinct form of writing that can be mentioned, involves writing through a fictional character. This experience is somewhat surprising. One "creates" a character and "creates" various situations in which a character might act. As one writes the story, the narrative, the life or thoughts of that character, a moment occurs when the character "takes over" and writes itself. Well, of course not *really*. But the phenomenological description could hardly be otherwise. After an hour of writing "through" a character in this way, one may pause to re-read only to feel startled on re-reading the passage, for example, to find that the character has done something that you, its creator, were not aware of. Or, one might wish in retrospect that the character "had decided" to do something else. Why is the writer not able to articulate the magic adhering to this process?[13] Why is this feeling of being taken over a part of writing fiction? How come it seems so unbelievable when it is attached to a real book, a real author. Thus Simenon talks this way about his writing and when we hear these words it is hard to believe him; hard to credit that his characters have "lives of their own." Such talk seems precious or false. OK, precious and false.

A second class of writing experience involves creating a character through whom to write theory. There might be two extremes to this experience. At the mundane end, although even here the adrenalin can be a little overwhelming, one recognizes that one is on deadline. Oh no, one thinks. "I" can't write this piece. Instead, one imagines who might be able to write this piece. And then one writes through that creation. Some people find this so much a part of the process that they name such characters. Kierkegaard is the obvious person to consider here. At the other end of this extreme one may find a fear so powerful that the writing ceases. One is like Madame Yeats. Writing but not writing. One becomes a vessel for something else entirely. This too, is unbelievable. We can hear these stories. We can understand them. We can make up additional stories about hysteria, about unconscious desires, about sexual repression.

Finally there is the writing experience that one might call absolutely clear. This is when you know exactly what is being written at every moment for the duration. In writing, there are times when there is an abstraction from the particulars of existence. We have experienced this: while writing a letter perhaps, or choosing adornment. I believe that if we have experienced something, even if we cannot explain it, it is necessary that the experience were possible. That is, there is some sense in which I must disagree with Wittgenstein when he says that: "When the answer cannot be put into words, neither can the question be put into words. The *riddle* does not exist. If a question can be framed at all, it is also *possible* to answer it" (Wittgenstein 1961, 6.5). So this magic moment which has no explanation is possible.

There is another issue that concerns me. When experiencing these kinds of writing, a very strange thing can occur. (Other sorts of experiences, some of them counter-intuitive in the extreme also produce this odd result.) The strange/odd thing in question is that when one is writing, one can, on occasion, realize that one has forgotten ones sex/gender. It is true! Who can deny this? There are moments of writing where one has forgotten and it is a strange sort of drag: one is who one is not. So this book is about ethics; it is about politics, but, it is mostly about gender politics. By the end of the book, I think it will be clear that ethics *is* politics which in turn *imply* gender politics. Letting beings be may very well turn out to include: letting ourselves go. This couldn't help but be political. Creating a mastery of context may turn out to include: always being in drag. This can't help but circumscribe a politics of gender: gender anarchy.

Chapter One

TRUTH

Heidegger has a theory of truth that is identical to whatever his ethical theory could be: namely, one must let things be to see them for what they are.[1] The ethical theory would have to be something like: freedom is acquiescing to the call of *dasein*.[2] A dilemma many have pondered is this, if Heidegger is right, then there can be no point in striving to the ethical or the political because his stance is antithetical to community building, or even community recognition. But on the other hand, if truth is much more than this and *ethos* is not an unavoidable given, then almost all of twentieth century theorizing doesn't even make sense. It is more likely that Heidegger's theory of truth is on the right track but that his inability to hook his reality up with human and lived life has to do with fear of becoming what he was. It is easier to see this if we think of his failure like this: in spite of Heidegger's anti-Cartesian stance, he is trapped in the equivalent of a Cartesian circle with respect to significant or meaningful others. Heidegger is arguably *the* philosopher of the twentieth century; as such, this radical anti-alterity must be acknowledged and addressed. It must specifically be addressed in this book because writing, as a mode of communication, presupposes others, others that recognize one and who desire recognition.

Heidegger gives us tomes of ontology. On the issues we need clarified he is virtually silent. He does not talk ethics nor politics. He talks and writes values in an overt way when

13

he talks about aesthetics. One wonders what this says about the twentieth century.[3]

1. *Truth as Vivid Imagination*

Heidegger writes using images. He uses representations, sometimes, in place of argument. The writing of significant philosophers is usually significantly different simply as writing. Their texts do not resemble insignificant texts. So, for examples, Socrates exhibits a lack, Kierkegaard an array of poets, Quine a rare facility with images, Wittgenstein an almost frightening directness.[4] In each of these cases the writing itself—something more than mere style—reveals something about the content being written. Heidegger's discussion of truth in *Being and Time* is at once a continuation of his deconstruction of western philosophy and a series of novel pronouncements on the nature of truth. In later works, Heidegger maintains the same criticisms of the traditional conception of truth but further elaborates the positive aspect of his doctrine. Alas, he offers but one convincing concrete example of truth (Heidegger 1977, pp. 143–188). The question Heidegger asks himself in "The Origin of the Work of Art" is "What is truth itself that it sometimes comes to pass as art?" (Heidegger 1977, p. 166). Heidegger's use of the work of art as an example of truth is neither incidental nor meaningful. Instead, I argue that it is some kind of fear, his fear, that deters a more straightforward account of truth. That is, Heidegger seems to be covering up things that he could have let be.

In section forty-four of *Being and Time,* Heidegger discusses the traditional conception of truth and the primordial phenomenon of truth; from there he proceeds to explain how the traditional conception of truth is derived from the primordial phenomenon. Finally, he describes "truth's particular being," namely: truth is that which is necessarily presupposed by Dasein. One is tempted to dismiss the project as outlined; it seems pedantic, arcane. We should try to re-member that Heidegger sees his project as a hearkening back through jargon. He views himself as sharing in (or forging) "the ultimate business of philosophy . . . to preserve the *force of the most elemental words* in which Dasein ex-presses itself, and to keep the common understanding of them from leveling them off to that unintelligibility which functions in turn as a source of pseudo-problems" (Heidegger 1962, p. 262).

The traditional characterization of truth is that it is an agreement. Within the tradition, this relation is both gen-eral and empty—hence for Dasein, for us, it is meaningless. Heidegger asks what else is presupposed in this relation and what is the ontological character of the presupposition. (If truth were general and empty we would not care about it and we would not work on it as a problem, we do, there-fore . . .) As long as we examine these questions within the traditional framework, says Heidegger, our answers will remain empty and general. We can substitute other rela-tions for agreement ("just as," "correspondence," etc.) but these substitutions do not allow us to reach any greater level of specificity. To reach a more specific level, we must additionally ask "What context of Being holds up the rela-tional totality?" That is, to put it another way, we must ask "What kind of Being allows the conglomerate of agreement relations to which we refer when we use the concept true to be intelligible?" This last question, says Heidegger, shows that the context of Being presupposes a duality of Being: the ideal or mental representation and the *real* Being. This separation of Being into levels causes epistemological prob-lems; the most important being "How do we ever connect these two levels of Being into a true judgment or piece of knowledge?"

Heidegger criticizes the bifurcation saying, "[i]f we go back to the distinction between the act of judgment and its content, we shall not advance our discussion of the question of the kind of Being which belongs to the *adaequatio* (Hei-degger 1962, p. 260). A new path must be forged, according to Heidegger, if we are to find the ontological basis for the *adaequatio*. And, this basis must be found if we are to discover the kind of Being which is possessed by truth. Heidegger hints at the direction his later work will take. He says: "The Being-true (truth) of the assertion must be understood as Being-uncovering" (Heidegger 1962, p. 261). But also, "The 'definition' of 'truth' as 'uncoveredness' and as 'being-uncovering', is not a mere explanation of a word" (Heidegger 1962, p. 263). Being true, then, *is* being uncovered. The foundation of this relation is possible only because of Being-in-the-world. This state of Dasein is the basis of the primordial foundation of truth. Heidegger is describing a reality and not, he hopes, talking only about words. And, by making this distinction explicit, he hopes to alleviate it.

One asks oneself at this point "What can he mean with all of this?" He has criticized those who allow common understanding to create and recreate pseudo problems. He describes a space, the clearing of Being, where most of us do not seem to be. He describes a place, in fact, where one could not be and know it with any degree of articulation. But, to dismiss Heidegger in this way is both too facile and too "false." Part of what is so difficult in understanding Heidegger's conception is that he does not hold what one would expect him to hold, given the theory of uncovering, that statements serve as the locus of truth. Statements, however are not that which Being uncovers, for Heidegger. Instead, the fact that we can make assertions *already* presupposes truth. Truth precedes its own expression not as concept but as grounding for true utterances, or feelings, or sightings. Heidegger equates this capacity with our being in the world. Dasein, by being in the world, is in truth, possessed by it, although not always possessing it. This brings us to what I take to be the most important question posed by Heidegger with respect to truth in *Being and Time*, namely, "What kind of Being is possessed by truth?"

Several concepts are central to Dasein's being possessed

by truth. First, truth cannot be without Dasein. Entities, once disclosed, do not come to be at that moment; instead, when an entity is disclosed we are aware of its already having been there. It was there but not in truth until disclosed. That is, until an entity is disclosed it has no meaning for us. Second, because we sense the entity's fore-presence at its disclosure we are moved to consider the nature of the presupposition of truth. Truth is presupposed in just this sense: without truth there can be no presuppositions at all. We could make no sense without the presupposition of truth. Here truth's essence could be seen as disclosed Being. The presupposition that Being is able to be disclosed precedes our being able to assert truths or falsehoods.

Heidegger augments his conception of truth in section 44. For Heidegger *"all truth is relative to Dasein's Being"* (Heidegger 1962, p. 270). If truth is relative to Dasein, is it not also relative to each dasein? Heidegger's answer is in the form of a rhetorical question:

> If truth has been correctly understood, is it in the least impaired by the fact that it is ontically possible only in the 'subject' and that it stands and falls with the Being of that subject? (Heidegger 1962, p. 270).

Heidegger doesn't think that truth is impaired. Instead, his explanation shows that the presupposition of truth shows truth to be dependent on the being of beings. One reason that this is so is that we cannot quarrel with what *is*. If truth is subject-relative, we cannot make it otherwise. Different interpretations arise in two general contexts: (1) when individuals will not let beings be and (2) when observations are such that the observer denies the ontological foundation of things. One could say that this begs the point of a *correct* interpretation. Still, we must remember that "a correct" is not the same as "the correct" interpretation. Heidegger is not going to allow us this sense of knowing. Every interpretation is *epistemically* as legitimate as any other.

2. *Aletheia: Zoon Anthropon: Life Becomes Us*

In 1964 Heidegger distinguishes *aletheia* (unconcealment) from *veritas* (truth).[5] This distinction helps in answer-
ing the question *Being and Time* side-steps, namely, "what
is the essence of truth?" The essence of truth is not quite
unconcealment. Aletheia, unconcealment thought as the
opening of presence, is not yet truth. This distinction is used,
although not mentioned explicitly, as early as 1935, and
Heidegger claims that the distinction is implicit in *Being
and Time*. The distinction with respect to art work (1935) is
that between earth and world. Earth is a grounding of world
as *aletheia* is the ground of truth. Is *aletheia*, then, the
essence of truth described in the lecture of that name? (Heidegger 1977, pp. 117–141). In that essay Heidegger says
that the essence of truth is freedom. To come in contact with
truth is to free oneself for the clearing. That is, truth is
possible because we are free to open ourselves to the inner
possibility of "correctness" in such a way that truth can be
recognized as a judgment. Is there a connection between
freedom and unconcealment?

If there is, it occurs surrounding the question: "How is
it possible to retain traditional values and symbols if there
are no standards by which to judge things true for everyone?" Heidegger's response is that "every valuing, even
where it values positively, is a subjectivizing. It does not let
beings: be. Rather valuing lets beings: be valued—solely as
the objects of its Doing" (Heidegger 1977, p. 228). In letting
beings be, then, we find truth because we throw off expecta-
tions through that letting them be. This is the freedom of
truth. "The bizarre effort to prove the objectivity of values
does not know what it is doing" (Heidegger 1977, p. 228). It
is the traditional side of the debate, according to Heidegger,
which will always turn relativist because it does not have
the "objectivity" to let things be. An example Heidegger uses
is one from ethics. He asserts that truth in ethics is the
finding of one's *ethos* (one's abode or dwelling place). We find

ourselves as what we are when we examine ourselves *before* the contemplation of theory or practice. What we find is the truth about ourselves. To theorize is to find ourselves in the untruth of the "they." Thus, Heidegger believes Sophocles to preserve *ethos* in a manner more primordial than does Aristotle.

How does a Heideggerian get around arbitrariness then? The "they" has been a fair standard of some things— better some might say than a radical subjectivity. One way around this is to notice Heidegger's self-defense as an acceptance or acquiescence to what is, to what must be. His language here indicates that his conception of Dasein's being in truth is one which must be regarded as a serious responsibility. For example, he states "Truth signifies sheltering that lightens as the basic characteristics of Being" (Heidegger 1977, p. 140). This passage involves images of caring and an implicit valuing of the worth of such sheltering. Nevertheless, images alone do not guarantee that, for instance, human communities will share each others's findings in the clearing. We would have no way of convincing someone else that their manner of letting things be was not "right." Early or late, the Heideggerian language does not satisfy. If it is honest, however, perhaps not achieving "philosophical" satisfaction is just beside any point.

To review, we see that truth ought not be defined in any way that is merely formal or empty. The analysis of truth must presuppose truth and truth's necessity for intelligibility. Truth *is* uncovering; truth *is* in the clearing of being; truth is freedom; truth is letting things be; truth is what is uncovered through the deconstruction of western metaphysics; truth is an overcoming of the dualism of the *adequatio*. All these descriptions of truth show the turn of truth around community: truth is *care*. But in this circle it is care itself that becomes formal and empty. What does this say about the twentieth century?

The purpose for my own pedantic and arcane retelling is that Heidegger's manner of arriving at his rejection of truth is at least as interesting as that which he says concerning it.

When truth is care, and when there is no grounded ethical theory, there is only subjective honesty. There are only "private" "relationships." Language is the house of being but no one is *at home for us* there. How come Heidegger doesn't just announce this?

3. *Phenomenological Imaging*

I mentioned the question "what is truth itself that it sometimes comes to pass as art?" Here is that question in its true surround.

> The art work opens up in its own way the Being of beings. This opening up, i.e., this revealing, i.e., the truth of beings, happens in the work. In the art work, the truth of beings has set itself to work. Art is truth setting itself to work. What is truth itself, that it sometimes comes to pass as art? (Heidegger 1977, p. 166).

What if Heidegger had been more forthcoming? What if he had told us what he meant? Some possibilities follow.

Possibility One. An artist creates a space in which the Being of beings is exposed. This revelatory process which gives us a truth of beings happens in the work. By work here, I mean either the working of the artist as s/he exposes indubitable ontological premises, or, the working of the viewer as s/he is struck by the undeniablity that the object of the painting *exists*. Of course there is some equivocation about object here. Within the art work itself, too, the truth of beings is at work in some necessarily quasi-mystical way, I guess. Art is truth is becoming is work. But as I say this, I recognize that I have stopped making sense. What is the truth that I am talking about?

Possibility Two. Art does not lie. It is honest about the intentions of its creators and re-creators. Eventually, the Being of the beings involved will be exposed—not! I mean: of the beings in the frame. Truth will come to pass. You can run but you can't hide. I am *not* a dualist.

Possibility Three. OK. Every picture tells a story. Every story is honest about its being a *real* story. The stuff *has just plain got to be there*. What is that stuff? What do I mean when I say "come to pass?"

The idea is there; the reader can write his or her own translation. The point, of course, is that there is something crucially false about the passage that surrounds that very important question. Why don't we re-write as if the problems of philosophy were real? Is this just some Wittgensteinian point thinking it is something else? How to find through writing that there is a falsity in the passage? A crucial one. We find that were we writing we could not talk about this third thing Art. It cannot be there. We find that were we writing this passage, such questions can always only be rhetorical. He begins to answer his own question, monolocutor, solocutor, lonely man, noting that, "the artist is the origin of the work. The work is the origin of the artist. Neither is without the other" (Heidegger 1977, p. 149). However, neither artist nor work is alone sufficient to the process of art-making for a third thing precedes them both—Art. Having established this starting point, "work" becomes problematic. Axes, clods of dirt, airplanes, death, judgment and works of art are all things. Heidegger wishes to distinguish between categories of things in an effort to let us know how the thingness of a work of art differs from other more homely things. He asserts that traditionally three sorts of things are accounted for: these are mere things, or those things which are bearers of traits; thing-structures, or the unity of manifold sensations, and, thing-concepts, or formed matter. Works are best defined in the last mode. He divides the last mode into three classifications: things, equipment and works. Despite this strangely, a-traditional, delineation, which shows in effect that mere things are just that, that equipment is usable and that works have something of mere thingness and something of concept thingness, Heidegger is still dissatisfied: "But we still know nothing of what we first sought: the things' thingly character. And we know nothing at all of what we really and solely seek: the workly character of the work of art" (Heidegger 1977, p. 164). When we find the workly character of the work of art, we will have found how truth can come to pass as art because works disclose beings in their unconcealedness.

But isn't this just exactly wrong? Doesn't everything have to disclose beings in their unconcealedness all the time for anything to be able to? Isn't the ultimately epistemic: "things are?" Or even "things *really* are?" Could his concrete example help?

On describing a van Gogh painting, Heidegger says: "This painting spoke. In the nearness of the work we were suddenly somewhere else than we usually tend to be . . . " (Heidegger 1977, p. 164). We are in the clearing and know that something has been "revealed" to us. Heidegger's concrete expression of this encounter with truth is one with which we are familiar. We know what he means when he states: "Van Gogh's painting is the disclosure of what the equipment, the pair of peasant shoes, *is* in truth. This being emerges into the unconcealedness of its Being" (Heidegger 1977, p. 164).

Art precedes both the being and the theory, the art work and the thing work. This line of thought parallels that found in the discussion of the presupposition of truth when making assertions. The notion of art's priority is connected with Heidegger's notions of earth and world which can be seen as truth standards which check each other with respect to their being in truth rather than untruth. In the following passage Heidegger combines his images in a way that sheds light, I think, on his stance against relativism in his work:

> What this word [earth] says is not to be associated with the idea of a mass of matter deposited somewhere, or with the merely astronomical idea of a planet. Earth is that whence the arising brings back and shelters everything that arises as such. In the things that arise, earth occurs essentially as the sheltering agent (Heidegger 1977, p. 169).

Earth is the ground for Dasein: it is the grounding for Dasein's thought. World is the creation which arises from such thinking. A world must derive from thinking about the earth—an arbitrary world will not then count as art work. "To be a work means to set up a world" (Heidegger 1977, p. 170). There is a strife between earth and world that allows creation to take place. "Setting up a world and setting forth the earth, the work is the instigating of this strife" (Heidegger 1977, p. 173). In the space which is created by the setting up of worlds, the unconcealedness of truth appears.

Truth, then, sometimes comes to pass as art because the artist, the viewer, and the thing meet in a world of "artistic space." The imagery of clearings, lightings, sheltering and space almost seduces us in this aesthetic context. Why then does the language jar us when it is used in more strictly epistemological contexts? Why is it so seemingly irresponsible to say: "Earth is the ground of the world; art is the ground of the art work; truth is the ground of sense; fear is the ground of writing." This is the direction in which I am going. Worlds, art works, sense, writing: these things reveal us in our thinking. We call this epistemology.

4. Truth Becomes Us: Literally

For Heidegger the ultimate analysis of truth is that truth becomes us. Truth is. Period. Literally. This is the ultimate leveler. It makes everything okay. The notion of reasonable discourse becomes meaningless. There is only force and strife.

5. Letting Sleeping Dogs Lie

I have a friend who refuses to read or write Heidegger. Perhaps you have seen her or him discuss this point on the net. S/he says that we shouldn't read or write or teach or study Nazis. S/he says we should let sleeping dogs lie.[5] A lot more is said in this regard. I guess the important point from persons who share this view is that there is nothing Heidegger can say in his defense: epistemically or ethically. Even aesthetically.

6. *All is not Lost*

Cixous has a theory of truth: she represents as immediate what has been mediated so thoroughly that the appearance of same could never be imagined as mediated. "One creature is worth as much as another. Another? The other! Ah, the other here is the name of the mystery, the name of You, the desired one for whom Clarice Lispector has written—all her books. The other to love. The other who puts love to the test: How to love the other, the strange, the unknown, the not-me-at-all? The criminal, the bourgeois, the rat, the cockroach? How can a woman love a man? Or another woman" (Cixous 1991, p. 140). Reread Cixous and put in here the counterbalance to Heidegger that allows movement. Introduce, without naming, the Hegelian influence, at work in/through you and be cleansed through Cixous.

Chapter Two

FEAR

New York City was freedom not because no one cared (no one did care) about something called humanity.... Not because no one cared about the things that didn't matter.... But because, for the first time, she was being given a way to be a person. To say other than *no*. Through work or the movement of the heart or of the imagination in the world. This material movement of the heart or the imagination, which is also the world, in this simultaneously angelic and rotten city, gave the worker fame (credentials) and formed a community not otherwise found in the world.[1]

To think against "values" is not to maintain that everything interpreted as "a value"—"culture", "art", "science", "human dignity", "world", and "God"—is valueless. Rather, it is important finally to realize precisely through the characterization of something as "a value" what is valued is robbed of its worth.[2]

When fear is characterized and catalogued, its value, as the mediating term toward a next stage of fear, is diminished. In fact in so thinking, so writing, so communicating about fear, the fear in question is felt, used by and passed over to a next stage. Fear makes us only say no; it keeps us from affirming work, imagination, the world. It keeps us from the truth of being in the world without mediation. But an obsession with the block toward affirmation can turn this one particular work into something which can appear to be the whole thing: which can lend itself to us as *life*. Nothing could be worse than this mistake. It makes it impossible to ever "acquiesce" or be blessed in Spinoza's sense. This is to say that if we cannot see our reaction formation against intense fear as a stage toward acquiescing in being, but instead view that formation as the fabric of a life, we will be hopelessly enmeshed in the emperor's new clothes. We are not even the foolish emperor; we would be the cloth of the non-existent wrap.

1. Uncovering Fear Involves Using Up Fear

Some philosophers are probably afraid of French philosopher Georges Bataille. Scarcely anyone else should be anymore. Many will say that women should be. It is well known that he and his work are misogynist, to put it politely. The very fact that it is well known mitigates against his power. What is frightening is that he is so appealing to the pop world. Techno-pop and the erotic novels just go together, by which I mean that I am not surprised when young friends and relatives tell me that they have recently read and "really liked" *Blue of Noon* or that the religious writings accurately describe what raving "means to me". Bataille is to post-industrial what Nietzsche is to psychedelic rock. His *stance* has been appropriated, changing the world but making Bataille himself hence forth innocuous, otiose. The June 1993 Mondo cover surely resonates with Bataille's readers. It is in these moments that the philosopher becomes us, literally, we breathe and speak him; computer images offer up his eyes. His *stance* is in the pop world and the origins of this entry are erased. The flat imagery of pop mirrors its a-traditional subject position. Pop is a stage in the progression of world history but it is not self-conscious of its movements.

My younger friends and siblings get their first Bataille fix from the bass player in Vicious Id or the drummer for No More Hoods. I find out about Bataille from a man who plays stand up bass in a jazz duo who is ABD in Political Economy. He gives me a novel and quotes Rimbaud on the flyleaf. My second encounter occurs through Jacques Derrida. He introduces Bataille into a space where we confront the fear of Bataille and in staring at it, eye to eye, use it up. That particular fear is used, partially stored for future meanings, and, as Bataille becomes popularized, a new fear arises. What will it be? Let us look at the movement created by Derrida's move toward the erasure of the fear of glissage: *differance*, reaction formation to *glissage*. An interesting way to approach this reaction formation is through the study of an overt appropriation of Bataille's Hegelian categories. Before I can do that coherently, it might be helpful to lay the academic background. This division between the popular and the academic is academic in the old sense. Derrida is certainly a popular figure. Not just in France. His work is more of a commodity than the recordings of, say, hard core band Flipper. For our purposes how Flipper and Derrida feel about this fact is irrelevant. (I mean: neither "want" to be "pop.") The distinction between popular and serious textual work seems conceptually hopeless to me, still, most of us can use the bogus distinction with ease. There are differences between Flipper and Derrida and we know what they are. Both produce products for consumption and for redemption. The products to be consumed by those who will redeem them by turning them into stars. But one entity produces products for institutionalized subjectivities and the other produces products for institutionally marginalized subjectivities. Implications of the distinction change the history of philosophy. That Nietzsche has been popularized has kept him from "serious philosophy" classes for years. (Same for Kierkegaard.) Now, the fact that he had been popular endears him to the purveyors of the canon.

The pertinent text is "From Restricted to General Economy: A Hegelianism Without Reserve."[3] This essay contains

Derrida's reading of Georges Bataille's relationship to Hegel with respect to several key concepts in Bataille's work. That the triad is Hegel/Bataille/Derrida is tremendously important. What is the accident of history that made Hegel the founder of semiotic materialism rather than Spinoza? It is dizzying to think Spinoza/Bataille/Derrida. In the essay, Bataille's discourse is said to reach a point where all Hegelian concepts (and hence the concepts of Western metaphysics) tremble and are dislocated but this point, once seen, reconfines itself to servitude and discursive meaning. This is not to say that nothing has happened. Bataille's contribution is to have shown that there is text and vision—that the conceptual/textual framework is not stable. That there is the opening of an *eye*. That this eye reinforces a gaze that literally disembodies women accounts in large part for the contribution being so "pop" popular at this juncture in cultural history.

What Bataille does to Hegel is to intensify Kojeve's notion of the violence of the dialectic to such an extent that dialectic was shaken apart. As is argued in *Prophets of Extremity*, absolute knowledge is traded for non-knowledge.[4] What Derrida does is to shove Bataille back into Hegelian dialectic by showing how his concepts in the end are in service of Hegel. All the while noticing (double position) that Bataille, like Artaud, like Mallarme and Sollers, made a huge advance by noticing play in and by language through rejecting the oppressive commitment to the immediacy of intuition. The title of Derrida's essay is thus a 'joke.' Hegelian economy is restrictive: Bataille's general economy is the Hegelianism without reserve: "General Economy in the first place, makes apparent that excesses of energy are produced, and that by definition, these excesses cannot be utilized. The excessive energy can only be lost without the slightest aim, consequently, without any meaning." (Derrida 1978, 270). In Hegel the loss is quantifiable and Spirit wants and needs less "stuff" as time goes by. However, the general economy of Bataille is restricted compared to Derrida's general economy which is really the Hegelianism without reserve pace Derrida. All of Bataille's categories are Hegelian. In other words, Bataille's economy is at once general and restricted economy. Except there is the opening of an eye with Derrida's "perhaps's" and his "and yet's." There is an opening of an eye with Bataille's certain laughter. He is not in fear in these moments because he is certain, he has no doubt.

Thrash music is also Hegelian. My back and forth between Bataille and Hegel, Derrida and Flipper, thrash music and Nietzsche *is* warranted. Philosophy is made scandalous with the intervention of Bataille; it is made subversive with the eruption of Foucault, of Butler; it is popular music since Nietzsche. Nietzsche writes of Wagner. Aristotle writes of tragedy. Heidegger, Holderin. Adorno, jazz. Late capitalist theory of Madonna. Thrash, hardcore, strike me as more true than the popular culture that is more traditionally theorized. I want these images to be mixed-up; I want us to consider the implications of philosophy in the world. I want us to remember that our words are not restricted to graphematic economies. We assign *Writing and Difference*. Someone reads Artaud and Bataille has a consequence. They leave college and start a band. How Bataille's eyes work themselves out concerns us. A younger relative has a friend who has a friend who acts Bataille out.

Thrash music is Hegelian. It recognizes itself as both ritual and as closed sign system. What is its laughter? Where will it get its "and yet's," its "perhaps" to unrestrict its restrictions. What is its "something left over," its "something worth fighting for?" Hard-core bulletin boards, concerts and events have more energy than arena commercial and mainstream music 'zines. Why? Are they one fraction of the new economy? Are they still on the eve of a new economy?

Derrida views Bataille's laughter as an instance of an opening toward excess. Can we read this seriously? When Derrida writes this is he thinking about . . . ? Well, he must be. Derrida's slipperiness is an instance of an opening toward excess as well. Why is Bataille important to this subculture while Derrida is not? Is it merely because Derrida does not write fiction? What in Bataille's writing is able to break through fear to its overcoming and its progeny, a new movement?

My first encounter with Artaud. I am in a big city. I have two friends with me and we are walking around. I see a text just lying on the ground. I stoop, pick it up. It is the largish Artaud, with the black and white photo on the cover. It is heavily read. It has not been accidentally dropped. It has been thrown down. I keep it. I still have it. Years later I read of his last performance. Of the tender treatment from Gide.

Ostensibly, Hegelian economy never has anything left over. It cuts off ecstacy, poetry, etc. This economy includes all the forms and resources of its exterior (present past future) and keeps hold of them by enunciating them. Economy is everything that is, but what is, is limited. On the contrary comes Bataille: the economic interpretation of history in the precise meaning of class struggle is already given in Hegel; Marx affirms the primacy of need. Bataille asks where do we go from here? How can I overcome these constants? I give up the certainty of meaning for the possibility of escape but in seeing this "out," I see that the loss must be kept in the economy for my utterances to have been possible and if it is kept there, then the loss has always already been there. We ought not to blind ourselves to the loss. We must open our eyes. Hegel has a blind spot. Bataille has an eye. Derrida points to the eye. And at this point we should all be laughing. There is something so obscene and so puerile in this discussion. It is so obvious. Is all of this obvious to Derrida then? What does he think when he rereads his essay now? And does the existence of thrash change his reading the way that his reading has changed them: each to each with no immediate connection?

Consciousnesses come together to get past a certain kind of dominance and submission in order that their work might have meaning for them. As the one consciousness looks at the other it is clear that "if it has not experienced absolute fear but only some lesser dread, the negative being has remained for it something external, its substance has not been infected by it through and through" (Hegel 1977, paragraph 196). What ever is other to us fills us with a dread that must be overcome. We are using up the fear opening ourselves to some new alterior opening. But do we only want to see? Don't we need more than eyes? Don't we want to touch? The dialectic of philosophy with popular culture is at the level of the eye. We watch, we theorize, we don't get dirty. As a consequence, we are only partially overcoming the fear. Each successive movement is partial. We are seriously disabled.

Bataille is laughing and thinking, look, I left the novels too. I understand touch. And Derrida on Bataille on writing centers around this issue of experiencing the other completely before a supersession is possible. Writing is a meaning creation that can contain the silence that points to the opening of the eye. Only one of two forms of writing can do this. The sovereign renunciation of recognition, while powerful, is not the sort of writing that will get us past a specific instance of fear. Only Bataille's sovereign form of writing that must interpret the servile complicity of speech and meaning can do this. Bataille's attempt to find a speech that maintains silence is a sliding and a risky one at that. Two things are risked: meaning and the loss of sovereignty. The sovereign operation retains something, namely, the urge for the relation of language to sovereign silence which, sadly, tolerates no relation. And yet. There needs to be such a relationship—subordinate significations to the operation which is a non-relation cannot but must exist. What Derrida has done is to reconstruct the system of Bataille's propositions on writing so that they are related to the trace. From the trace, it is a quick move back to the middle term. Philosophy has reassimilated its crucial part. It is one body again, only this time with an eye turned outward. An eye protected by the entire corpus.

Later, in "The Ends of Man," Derrida says that there are three tremblings within French Theory. The second of these is the strategic bet. It constitutes a radical trembling which can only come from outside and which takes two forms (a) to exist or deconstruct without changing terrain and (b) to decide to change the terrain in irruptive fashion. By tying Bataille to the trace, the two form come together for a moment. Bataille is reconstructed and not deconstructed because he is capable of being read without retrospective teleology. The space of writing is major sovereignty. Bataille has form and torment, or he does not tolerate the distinction between form and content. Everything in Bataille's writing is a relating of all conceptual content to the sovereign operation. Meaning is exhausted.

Are we on the eve of economy? Yes. The communities that are rising up have writing behind them. And who cares where they get their Hegel in the end? If they get Hegel, they can subvert the dominant paradigms, becoming economists in the true sense of the word. Using fear up, by looking at it in the face, forces new positions. These new positions terrify anew; on occasion, however, a form will be thrown up that is sovereign without domination. There are no more writings that are not everywhere. Everyday I communicate with thousands of people on the net and hundreds more as I walk down the street expressing my allegiance to certain social formations in the way I move and the way I dress. And if you don't do the first, you certainly do the latter. These communications probably still carry the taint of domination. That writing need not, we have just seen that, gives hope that community interaction need not. But it is clear that it will not be enough to say, as so many of us have in so many contexts, that we are going to suspend hierarchal thinking for this or that meeting. (Of course this is not what we say, but it is what we mean.) Maybe we need to experience domination and submission in various forms before overcoming them for those forms. We cannot pretend them away. That we think we can shows how little we know about the workings of our bodies. We need to experience the fear, in order to overcome it by using it up. The semiotic economy, however, is a real one, a material one and using it up means literally playing it out.

2. But Fear Cannot Be Used Up[5]

Of course, neither fear, nor anything else, can be completely used up. One thing we must face is the question "What will we be if we let go?" Perhaps even more to the point we might ask "Do we want to let go?" It is easier to turn, again, to theory. Irigaray says of Nietzsche that:

> He [Nietzsche] is mask and blinded eye. Once his creation is realized, he lives it. And nothing else. There is no other night that might allow him to continue to make himself flesh. No other to set the limits of his corporeal identity with and for him, putting his latest thought into the background so a new one can be born.
> The sacrifice he makes to the Idea is inscribed in this—that he preferred the Idea to an ever provisional openness to a female other. That he refused to break the mirror of the (male) same, and over and over again demanded that the other be his double (Luce Irigaray 1991, p. 187).

This passage captures Nietzsche in so many ways that this, in itself, is terrifying. At first. Irigaray captures Nietzsche. Nietzsche lives his creation; he is in truth. But a partial truth. The eye is blinded; the being is masked. He cannot get around the Idea. What is the nature of the refusal? The refusal is to the openness of the female other, in a sense, however, this female other includes not just the female corporeality and the female proliferation of ideas. Nietzsche is refusing all but the male Idea. He has refused male corporeality as well. The overcoming of fear can be quite conscious through discipline—this is the way that Nietzsche writes these moments. The overcoming of fear, however, can be quite unconscious. One can simply let oneself be in the night besides which there is no other. Bataille's eye, his solar anus, how can we shrink from saying this, forces us to look at what we have refused. It is so much. This discourse that does not let us touch each other or ourselves. Panopticon, the eye magnified, the technology of the eye, turns speculum, and finds the female body literally transparent. It will take a long time to find ourselves.

A reader could be asking, what really is she writing about here? I am thinking about what I am writing really. Sometimes when I read and ask myself the question that some of you are asking at this moment, I just can't tell. Are we talking about discourse? text? Is the body a text? In the sense that it is a text are we really talking about penises and vaginas, real ones? Are we talking about actual speculums, actual panopitcons? It is hard to know. I have been talking about bodies being literally transparent. The female body is literally unprotected from the gaze of the speculum and the panoptican and Bataille's eye. It is exposed by this new theorizing.

Irigaray forces us to analyze ourselves into positions where we *can* be the sorts of things that can in turn subvert the subject positions that refuse our breaking through. Hers is the body work to Bataille's glissage, or conceptual work. I do not mean to suggest that Irigaray is somehow making material Bataille's conception. In fact, given the intellectual history in which we find ourselves such a reading of Irigaray denies the real force of what she has done. She erupts through the texts with bodies and body parts and says: look at this. The vision that has underlain Western metaphysics privileges rigid symbolic orderings. Let's redo everything we see with touch. And this means not just doing theory and just writing. It means, among other things, writing past dominance and submission such that we can wear a body that communicates itself as past dominance and submission in as many places as possible.

I must note that I find k.d. lang much more interesting than Madonna. Insofar as we can see the economy's possibility she is the eve. I do not mean to denigrate Madonna by this comparison. As if "I" could matter here.[6]

I have mentioned community in this overcoming. The community at a Madonna concert is different from that at a k.d. lang concert. There is overlap but the feeling is different.

My use of community here may resonate poorly with other fellow communitarians. Like Bill Martin, I believe that we need to take our cultural structures where we can find them. (I feel certain that he, however, would disagree with my use here.) Still, in these arenas, these clubs, we come to see ourselves interacting. These communities seem to be neither paper nor virtual. Following my reasoning to this point, however, no community could fail to be one or the other. (And of course virtual communities depend on paper ones.) There is some sense in which certain musical communities are "merely" virtual as opposed to "really" virtual. (You see this truth thing is quite easy isn't it?) A "merely" virtual community is one where there is shared data but no interaction between those that share the data. Thus, many of us purchase, for example, house music. The act of purchasing and consuming those products does not form a virtual community by the simple fact that there is no interconnectedness between those persons doing the similar sorts of things—even dancing a certain step, alone in one's home. What is probably most commonly called hard-core has a community that can be virtual—shared electronic zines, postings of concerts, and, can be paper—through hard zines and interactive print in general. Remarkably, there are communities that attach themselves to hardcore that are neither paper nor virtual—but derivatively both in the sense just described. I think that the best way to examine these communities is from a Hegelian perspective for reasons noted when discussing Bataille. These communities share a sense of dread of some other, and also an inferior copy of nationalism (or regionalism) best understood through the bad Hegel.

As I write this sentence, my child is ten months old. She can recognize melodies and on occasion reproduce them. She cannot recognize or reproduce sentences. Perhaps, music is the first writing we do—the first communication. All my first communications to her were melodic. I understand that this anecdotal noticing on my part may not even warrant the "perhaps" above; still, it seems as if the urge to order which finds itself in writing is present in the need to make music, to remember it, to reproduce it. My students may have trouble with remembering an argument from Kant or Hume; most of them can recite genealogies of their hundred or so favorite bands with no problem complete with exegesis of the change in themes (both musically and socially) from one incarnation of the band to the next. Perhaps, music underlies any ability to write or read. My students read very well depending on where I decide to examine them.

Some of you will probably all agree with me that the music of George Clinton is joyous. One of the most amazing things in recent mass culture was the marriage of funk and grunge (complete with wedding dressed, male, rhythm guitarist) on the television set. Grammy's. 1993. Red Hot Chili Peppers and George Clinton. Amazing. Awe inducing. Joyous. And, yes, of course there are gender troubles. With a wedding dress no less. Some music is intense without being joyous.

"Death . . . is of all things the most dreadful, and to hold fast what is dead requires the greatest strength" (Hegel 1977, paragraph 32). Mass culture has also produced a music that is not particularly joyous. It does not even try to be. It is interesting because it is at once a-traditional and political this bad Hegelian music, this death steeped dissonance. Sometimes this music is called hard- or speed-core. Sometimes it is called post-punk. Sometimes it is called death metal. It is a very fast, rarely melodic, rarely acoustic and frequently violent music. Sometimes it is called thrash, my personal favorite. The classifications glide around, allegiances within the communities glide around. How to describe the music? It is fast, not very melodic and amplified electrically much more than other forms of music. The music is political in its content but there is no "party line" for the genres. Some thrash bands are fascist, some are pacifist; some death metal bands are neo-nazis and some are anarchists and some are militantly apathetic. Some are what is called straight edge (str8-edge)—they do no drugs and are generally vegans as well. Some are violently anti-racist. At a recent Murphy's Law concert in Philadelphia, the band made it clear that they would personally take care of any racially suspect incident. Regardless of the political stance the bands are mostly white and the audiences are too.

The music is a-traditional in the sense that it tries to escape any but its most immediate musical roots. It might be better to say it is "unhistorical" in Nietzsche's sense.[7] Thus, there is amplified guitar but rarely any allusion to an old blues or rhythm and blues riff. Thus, there is punk stance but rarely a connection to punk music of the seventies. The music appropriates in a similarly haphazard fashion from commercial rap music. Quick citing, no historical linking, reggae here, rap here, even joking references to disco—in moments.

This music is Hegelian. It seems to view the world from a naive Hegelian standpoint. While some of the musicians must have come in contact with Hegel's philosophy, probably most have not.[8] The anarchist bookstores which are usually in the neighborhoods of the clubs where performances are held, carry Semiotext(e) lines, psychedelic music lines, hardline buttons and bumperstickers and sometimes Bataille. "Popular" culture reflects commonly held beliefs. What these genres reflect is the free-flowing Hegelianism of the age. Whether they are conscious or not of Hegel or any of the weirder Hegelians (e.g., Bataille), their focus on death, violence, and loss is best understood under Hegelian religious/artistic categories. A Hegelian reading enables us to read the texts without making prescriptions about the music, the followers of the music, or the culture that has this music as its most representative art form. That this is a representative art form implies nothing about what one ought to listen to or turn one's attention toward.

It is harder and harder to be a straight Hegelian. Hegel's ambiguity seems to force tacit prescriptions. One still hears the debate: "Is Hegel an atheist or *the* theist of all time?" "Is he a radical or reactionary or a proto-fascist?" Take the term a-traditional again. The original meaning of "traditional" was "surrender" or "betrayal." "A-traditional, " then is that which is neither traditional nor anti-traditional, but in *our* sense and not in the original, or traditional sense. Beyond acquiescence and reaction. This a-traditionalism has made observers believe them to be more subversive than they are. The music is an accurate representation of the culture from which they arise: culturally illiterate, non-root oriented, a-traditional. These genres do not represent fringe movements: they represent this historical period accurately. They are some of our "religious" artists.

Death and war cover up the need and desire for communication. The music offers a place where it seems that one is relating to others just as war offers a political stance that appears as if it is diplomacy. I was at a hardcore concert the night that Clinton ordered Iraq be bombed. In spite of what I've just said, I am glad that I was there. The news made its way into the hall to booings and screaming. Hegel and thrash have correctly described modernity. The wide spectrum of political views expressed by the groups within our genres is evidence that the most serious problem with Hegel's manner of doing philosophy is that it cannot take sides. Part of what this means is that there is not really "popular" "culture" because if reality is as Hegel describes, then there can be nothing like the consensus about meanings or values in which, for examples, Habermas and Rorty believe.[9]

The emphasis these genres place on megadeath, the violence of death, and the finitude of life are not echoes of anything in the metal that precedes them. Why should anyone be interested in this motley group of musicians and their admirers? In the *Phenomenology* Hegel says "that it is *perceived* or *heard* means that its *real existence dies away*; this, its otherness, has been taken back into itself; and its real existence is just this: that as a self-consciousness. Now, as a real existence, it is *not* a real existence, and through this vanishing it *is* real existence" (Hegel 1977, paragraph 508). Artists, like philosophers, can only see what is in sight. And in much of US culture, that means *not* seeing the *tradition*, not seeing what is and what is becoming.

Death metal is religious in the sense that it comprises a

ritual for its members that is meaning-creating; it explains certain problems for its listeners, and it requires certain allegiances both mental and physical. Thrash is religious in all three of these senses as well but thrash offers comic explanations. It goes beyond the tragic or the simple ritual. At first glance it would seem that in terms of religion in the form of art, these descendants of metal and punk would be best classified in that area that Hegel calls the "cult". He says that "the movement of the two sides constitutes the Cult . . . a movement in which the divine shape *in motion* in the pure feeling element of self-consciousness, and the divine shape *at rest* in the element of thinghood, mutually surrender their distinctive characters, and the unity which is the Notion of their essence achieves an existence" (Hegel 1977, paragraph 714). The two sides of movement (speech of the oracle and the statue or icon) show what is sacred, or most valued, both in motion and at rest. The motion and rest mutually surrender into each other as meaning. A death metal concert does this through the inert representations (back-drop, massive wall of speakers) and the motion that has to be experienced to be believed. Voi Vod for instance is well known for their guitarist who plays miraculously fast all the while thrashing his black as ink ponytail into an impossible blur. Behind this performance is the icon, the Voi Vod flag. During this process "this Being [whose essence, the unity of the one and the other] descends from its universality, through the mediation of the Cult, into individuality, and thus unites itself with reality" (Hegel 1977, paragraph 716). Nothing counts but the blur of sound and the blur of bodies. Hegel perfectly describes the unity that descends on the audience during a good show. Each person is with everyone else at the peak of his or her individuality. It could not have happened *alone*, nor could it happen without concrete individuality. The unity is created in the event; minutes earlier in the parking lot, or on the sidewalk waiting to be let in, there is no unity whatsoever.

It is not enough that this unity be created. The members of the cult must make some sort of effort to show their devotion to the cult. Hegel says that "the act of the Cult itself begins therefore with the pure *surrender* of a possession which the owner, apparently without any profit whatever to himself, pours away or lets rise up in smoke" (Hegel 1977, paragraph 718). Most fans surrender themselves to the music. But this is not all. As numerous commentators have pointed out, heavy metal is pretty much a working-class phenomenon. (What some refer to as plastic metal or poseur metal is not working-class.) Young working class persons in this country are massively underemployed. The financial sacrifice in being a fan is immense. At one concert I remember the lead singer telling us how grateful he was to us for buying tickets because he knew how hard it was to scrape money together like that. (It is a point of pride with hardcore groups not to allow venues to overcharge for tickets. Thus, most hardcore groups and fans are disgusted by Lollapalooza for example.) Furthermore, those persons who are provided for financially at home generally face parental disapprobation for their adopting this particular musical lifestyle. It is a sacrifice for most people to be at the shows and for the "actors" to give their lives to it. There is virtually no hope of becoming a star. Being a star destroys what the whole scene is about.

As Hegel shows us, the new moment contains the old. As history progresses, death metal is absorbed by the next category. "The nation that approaches its god in the Cult of the religion of art is the ethical nation that knows its state and the actions of the state to be the will and the achievement of its own self" (Hegel 1977, paragraph 720). Herein lies the discrepancy between the proto-Christian cults that Hegel is describing and the death metal "cults". We are in a different phase of the dialectic. There is no ethical nation that knows its state. There are ethical communities that know their constitution. The state no longer has either "god" or "art." These things take place in communities separate from the "state". The state "knows" this. It tries to impose its "god" and its "art" but it fails at this because it has violated its trust too many times. Peruse any 'zine or even trade publication which concerns itself with death or thrash. Requisite to the genre is absolute trust between the artist and the fan. Good guitarists are said to be god and "to rule". If they are found not taking the lifestyle seriously they are labeled poseur and then dropped. Sometimes literally, a person who turns coat will be dropped in a stage dive. The fans and the artists enter into a communal relationship, supplanting that which might have occurred with the State. Al Gore's near stage dive at the Democratic election night celebration (1992) was an absolutely incredible moment. Al Gore, thrashing all around. Incredible. The cheapening of every sacred act into a sound byte threatens to destroy the very idea of community.

Now what is the nature of this image? Al Gore, husband of Tipper Gore, president of a censorship group which targets hardcore and rap, stage dives.[10] (Or appears to, for image's sake only appearance counts.) "Communication" here requires beings who have put their being at stake—have placed it at death. It is a joyless "sacrifice," a slavish dependency on structure a failure to really communicate. Death is not the negation of negation—it is nothing—and so nothing is preserved. Communication, in this new sense, is to talking what dreaming is to the dreamwork. Every communication will be a projection to one or more others of the sacrifice of one self to the selves of expression. One can communicate politics to others in moments in the world but one can only say as part of a rational narrative something like "then we decided to adopt the second plan". One almost wants to say that if a political strategy can be explicated in a clear fashion, it is because it has failed. A clearcut struggle that can be fought head-on by joining the appropriate "culture" or "community" is necessary to human beings. If no struggle is entered, the self patiently waiting to be filled by content becomes sacrificed to an oppressor instead of being overridden by an acting self. More importantly, if a strategy embarked on is a strategy against existing hierarchy and authority that controls the self, the strategy will have an effect on that power source which is as difficult to theorize as the moment of change in political action. The rich and diverse cultures that surround non-assimilable forms of music are an example here. This music has as its most important feature that it is a-traditional and that it can't be "developed". It is its own end. No future strategies are promised; the manner of the culture's existence and its recuperative powers necessitate making temporary oppositional selves. These small cultures chip away at the power source, most successfully when they are unnoticed because they are mistaken for variants of the power source. The music that sings to the vestigial "state" selves likes to think that it encompasses all variations. Death "knows" better.

Thrash music is better classified with comedy, the third stage of the section on religion in the form of art. Hegel says that "the Spirit of the community is thus in its immediate consciousness divided from its religious consciousness, which declares, it is true, that *in themselves* they are not divided, but this merely *implicit* unity is not realized, or has not yet become an equally absolute being for self" (Hegel 1977, paragraph 787). This brings us back to death and politics again. Let's look at Hegel on the community and politics and how this explains thrash music.

Hegel says "The community can only maintain itself by suppressing this spirit of individualism, and, because it is an essential moment, all the same creates it and, moreover, creates it by its repressive attitude towards it as a hostile principle. However, this principle, being merely evil and futile in its separation from the universal end, would be quite ineffectual if the community itself did not recognize the power of youth, as the *power* of the whole" (Hegel 1977, paragraph 475). This passage is from the section on the ethical order in *The Phenomenology of Spirit*. The power of young men is said to be that which must be used by those older and wiser members of the community. Women, who represent the irony of life, also are those who try to keep youth from hooking into the universal. Instead, women try to keep their male youth tied to the particular, or to family life. Hegel believes that there will be resistance to this pull away from the universal. Such resistance manifests itself on occasion as war. On other occasions the resistance manifests itself as art.

The weary dynamic of male war and culture set up against the female hearth has not been completely supplanted. There is no love/hate relationship with women in Hegel. There are only descriptions of exclusions and resentments. Thrash mirrors this. It is not surprising that in spite of gains by women in many areas, these gains are not mirrored in many popular cultures. Instead what is mirrored is the latent desire of exclusion and the latent resentment. Because the mirror is art, it brings to surface what is latent. Thrash is not unique in this respect. Popular cultures do very little that is more progressive with respect to women than does thrash.

Another Hegelian description of the politics of death, viz., war, is the notion that war is necessary for firm governance. The concept of diplomacy is never sufficient to this end because diplomacy does not hold fast to death. Hegel says: "The *community*, the superior law whose validity is openly apparent, has its real vitality in the government as that in which it has an individual form. . . . In order not to let them become rooted and set in this isolation, thereby breaking up the whole and letting the [communal] spirit evaporate, government has from time to time to shake them to their core by war. By this mean, the government upset their established order, and violates their right to independence, while the individuals who, absorbed into their own way of life, break loose from the whole and strive after the inviolable independence and security of the person, are made to feel in the task laid on them their lord and master, death" (Hegel 1977, paragraph 453). The hopelessness of thrash shows it to be one step beyond Hegel. Death *has* supplanted diplomacy; it seems very difficult to see how we can sublimate the megadeath of our culture with diplomacy now.

Revolution is the flip side of war. What war does for the governance of states, revolution does for the governance of the anti-state. On death and revolution Hegel says: "The sole work and deed of universal freedom is therefore *death*, a death too which has no inner significance or filling, for what is negated is the empty point of the absolutely free self. It is thus the coldest and meanest of all deaths, with no more significance than cutting off a head of cabbage or swallowing a mouthful of water" (Hegel 1977, paragraph 590). If Hegel is correct that "what is called government is merely the *victorious* faction, and in the very fact that its being a faction lies the direct necessity of its overthrow; and its being government makes it, conversely, into a faction, and [so] guilty" (Hegel 1977, paragraph 591), then thrashers are correct to withdraw, to some extent, from politics. What could the point be? I feel obliged to say that this despair is not mine. I am arguing that if one were a-traditional in the sense I have described and mirroring the state of the world in a pre-self-conscious manner, then it makes perfect sense to conclude that one's politics are merely a matter of deciding whom one should kill.

In an economy that cannot do away with sovereignty, there is no way to either ignore death or to give it its proper conceptual space. Death is there as unthinkable. At the same time, however, the only way to remember that one is alive is to almost die, or alas, to almost kill. Thus, the dancing that accompanies this music which is literally risky. And the streets outside after the shows that are literally risky. And by extension other dancing, other streets. And by extension other beating, other streets. Unleashed violence is so much a part of our repression that we are honestly not surprised by brutal racial beatings, by gay and lesbian bashing, by confessions that ones most intimate relationships are at root violent. As I write this we find that Clinton has betrayed one of his most loyal constituencies.

One of the things many of us like about hardcore is the inevitable bruising. The juxtaposition between the last paragraph and this is brutal. Hardcore moshing, when overcrowded, is very much like a tame, group s&m experience. It is not very serious; it is not particularly mature. There is trust necessary for the dancing and if the trust is violated, the persons involved would suffer serious injury. If the trust is maintained, minor pain is the reward.

War appears to be inevitable. Death, of course, is. The same facts, the same methods yield radically different political stances but they amount to the same thing: death before life. Popular culture has become a disjoint series of popular cultures which produces a-traditional persons. The politics of a-traditional persons can only be a random choice between violent options. This is the world in which the creators of the rising generations "popular" "culture" find themselves. This is how they see and touch.

What would happen if thrash or hardcore became more traditional? Would its inherent violence dissipate? I think that it would and that this direction is a likely one if the fear of finding a place in a world which mirrors their sameness back to them can be overcome through using it up against it.[11]

3. Overcoming Fear in Moments[12]

Part of our fear is seeing death. Part of our fear is seeing our bodies. Part of our fear is becoming, literally, our bodies. George Clinton says free your mind and your ass will follow. Summing up everything. When the fear of death and our bodies-toward-death are acknowledged and lived, that fear is used up, the energy thereby released needs some focus. We make new bodies with mysteries we cannot penetrate. We make our minds infinitely large. At any moment, many of us can tap into a seemingly infinite amount of immediate information. We have bodies that we cannot possibly ever know: the body that can wittingly or unwittingly erase the life's work of another by the writing of electronic bombs; the body that harbors diseases that cannot be detected; the body whose power extends to infinity. We have deaths that seem increasingly meaningless. If categories glide, if body boundaries are created, then the information storage we direct is as much us as the little finger we use to seduce an old friend.

Foucault knows this, and yet as he walks into a room, he is not freed in mind or ass. He is beyond that now. Trying to comprehend this new situation. The room is noisy. Loud music of a certain kind is playing. It is not good music. There is an unpleasant smell in the room; the room is redolent of sweat that would have smelled good just yesterday. His glasses are uncomfortably heavy on his nose. Foucault's desire for something fine to drink will probably not be fulfilled in this particular room. Perhaps, he thinks, I will just nurse a beer. He is proud of this colloquial thought. It makes him less strange, less alien, less foreign. His head is uncomfortably heavy on his body. He wants to talk. He wants more than talk. He also wants to think out loud for someone; he wants to be less strange. Nietzsche is already in this room. He is nursing a dark beer. He is tired but not incapacitated. He is thinking, it is uncanny; I am not home for a change; I am not *at work*; I am not having a headache. I may even have a chat with someone. I may even proffer myself as a partner for some body work. He thinks that perhaps he is using this expression correctly but he cannot be certain of this.

Foucault notices the older man sitting at the bar. He is not intrigued. He must go to the bar to order the beer he will nurse and, as he approaches the bar, the older man turns and Foucault thinks, ah, at last we meet. I feel as if we know each other. I feel as if I know you to the point of identification with you. I feel as if we could really talk. As if we could confide in one another our particular subject positionings and that in so doing, we may very well discover something; something important. Nietzsche, of course, does not know who this young man is. In fact, neither would have recognized himself. Frozen in time as they are in that subject position in which they felt most at home. In Nietzsche's case it is not a subject position, he ever *really* filled; in Foucault's case it is the subject position created by the gaze of the sister. The much loved sister. Foucault sits next to the old man; for this old man, I will sit even here, at the bar.[13] Foucault sits. He says, "It has been said of me that I am always 'on the move, alone, secretive.'" He says, "It has been said of me that I distrust 'the marvels of interiority'" (Blanchot 1969, p. 68). Nietzsche shifts his position in order to get a better glimpse of this young man wishing he could ask him who he is. Perhaps he has read this man's work. Or perhaps he is one from the popular culture infiltration, Rush Limbaugh? A male lesbian? He doesn't say anything. Instead he is thinking, in silence. He thinks, "Need I say after all this that in questions of decadence I am *experienced*?" (Nietzsche 1969, p. 223). He thinks, this young man does not know how much I know. He thinks, I do not have to prove myself in this regard.

Foucault cannot be similarly introspective. He says, "there is a conflict in me and about me concerning where such conflict could even *be*". Nietzsche attempts to discern why this claim is something which clearly instills great pride in the speaker. He thinks to himself, perhaps this is just one of the echoes, what did they call it, noise? Foucault says, "It has been said of me that 'only at a certain point in European history did the author . . . begin to see himself as a creative individual who, in his work, gives expression to his interior subjective richness. The great master of such analysis was, of course, Foucault'" (Zizek 1989, p. 174). "That master," the youth says, "is me".

Nietzsche says nothing. He thinks, au contraire, mon frere. And why does he mumble so? He must be a recent translation, none of those knowing enough languages to use any of them with care. Scandalous. Still, he is silent. He is getting a headache. A pounding sensation behind his left eye. And why not, he thinks, with regard to the headache. The stomach will come next. And why not? I am not being sufficiently rude. I must cease. Being silent. Still. It *is* hard.

Foucault is oblivious to the silence of his friend. He says: "Too bad we can't have Heidegger here too. You know, I know Heidegger, as I do you, but I will not discuss him" (Foucault 1989, p. 326). Nietzsche knows he has read this

man. He had read this reference to Heidegger and to himself
prior to reading Heidegger so the man's name starts with A,
B, C, D, E, F, G, or H through Heidegger. He remembers
Heidegger very well indeed. He becomes aroused remembering those books, dog-in-manger-roused; of this man, he is
jealous. He says, "Look". Foucault looks surprised. Nietzsche says again, "Look". And then, "Listen". They motion for
another round in silence. Then, Nietzsche speaks. Foucault
feels as if this is a gift and somewhere he feels something
like gratitude.

"Heidegger may have understood me. It appears that
you believe that you have understood, or known, me. Bataille surely did. You three. Bataille is a bridge. He was a
bridge for love. It was a bridge for love that was required,
don't you see? And Bataille made that bridge. Irigaray loved
me. So, that is one thing. That is one thing to say."

Foucault feels oddly let down. So this, he thinks, this is
the man, this Nietzsche. This is not what I had anticipated.
Perhaps it doesn't work; perhaps in *real*, he would be, well,
more *real*. Foucault immediately senses a rush of self-loa-
thing at these dualist and essentialist thoughts he is having,
a rush as if from niacin. Still, Nietzsche seems so, well, not
heavy so much, but certainly non-light; Nietzsche is supposed to be gay and light. Is it possible that Irigaray *really*
read Bataille? The way *he* has? He doesn't know. He realizes
that he has never thought about this. Foucault is silent. He
is thinking, along with these thoughts of underwhelment *re*
Nietzsche, that little bastard. That cretinous little bastard—
the bastard in question being, of course, Bataille who has
had to ruin *everything*. Nietzsche is speaking. His voice is
raspy. He says,

"A second item of importance. A second thing to say. If
one says 'thought of thoughts' with no irony attached to
that saying, this sort of thing stems from incomplete thinking. His pre-eminence philosophically notwithstanding,
Heidegger must have been a silly little man. He writes of

my 'literary remains' again with no sense of irony (Heidegger 1984, p. 71). He writes of Zarathustra as the snake
and the eagle (Heidegger 1984, p. 232). He discusses me
but doesn't know me."

Foucault is decidedly excited. He is feeling like discussing power and more. He is a-tingle with potential discussions. He is in the mood for a walk, for setting rules, for
assuming positions. He makes as if to speak but Nietzsche
raises a hand, warningly, Foucault thinks. Well, Foucault
thinks, after all, he *is* Nietzsche. After all. Foucault thinks,
"Still it is interesting that I acquiesce to this hand motion so
quickly." At the same time he is thinking repetitively: "We
are both such stars!" For a moment this latter thought em-
barrasses him. Then he thinks, a petulant expression rising,
"But it is true. We are! We *are* stars!" Nietzsche sees this
expression and not being privy to the thought which gives
rise to it, finds it endearing, nearly sweet.

Nietzsche has raised his hand. He has signaled for silence. He speaks. In speaking he says, "Bataille is the bridge
to love. You may wonder what love has to do with it?" Foucault, misunderstanding, shakes his head, no, he understands the love thing. Nietzsche does not see the nod. He
continues, "There is a minor philosophical figure, but a very
interesting one, who writes genealogies, archaeologies, in
short, who does the detail of my abstract work." Foucault
shifts uncomfortably but not without pleasure; *this* is more
like it. "This philosopher, French, I think, from *France*, believes that pleasure and its satisfaction became rarified
through an over-abundant attention to desire. He fills in the
details of this becoming. Very interesting work, if a little
pedantic." Nietzsche pauses to clear his throat, tries to look
into the face of the young man seated next to him. The young
man is apparently finding a great deal to notice in the dregs
of his cup and so cannot return this gaze. "Well, he asks all
the right questions, for instance, concerning bodies, he asks
are they good? are they bad? Showing again his rather

dogged devotion to myself, which pleasures me as you might imagine." Foucault does not like this allusion to himself. He makes again as if to speak, and again, Nietzsche raises his hand. These rules, Foucault thinks, they keep me in bondage. These rules he thinks, they all come from him. Where is the trust?

Nietzsche speaks again and in speaking, he says: "So. He asks are these bodies we have, these necessary existientiels, by the way, you seem like a pomo, is that the correct usage of that piece of Heidegger?" Foucault nods curtly. His rage comes in and out. "Good. Well, these necessary existientiels can only be something other than good or bad if they are constituted from within, constituted as objects of pleasure, or not, that part irrelevant obviously." Foucault interrupts, "Not *obviously*. Not just *obviously*. Not everyone can see that bodies are self-constituted also." Nietzsche ignores this childish outburst. But he does change the subject. He says, "Since we've been here I've noticed that we are only with philosophers. You're new but you certainly appear to be one of us. But there are several persons with whom I wish to speak: Lou, for one, but also Luce. Do you know them? Do you know where I might find them?" Foucault cannot believe what he is hearing. "You mean Lou Salome? Well, she *is* a girl!" And the other one, Irigaray, is *alive*!"

Foucault walks into a room. He looks around for Spinoza but sees that yet again "Mazel" has decided to spend the day alone writing. Oh, God, there is never anyone to talk with anymore. Foucault cannot understand why they still want to write. He has tried on occasion and it seems silly, pointless. They are all here. I would have thought, he thinks, I would have thought that we would all be so glad to be with one another. We would have been so happy to talk and to fuck. But, oh, no, we have to keep these ridiculous schedules, this urge to produce, this denial of living in time right now. Why? There is nothing here forcing their hands; no possible recognition, no fear of getting it wrong. Even more importantly, there is no explanation or possible explanation for why they do it. Foucault had always believed that if there were such a place as this[14] there would be no possibility of communication. Each subject would have been constructed so differently that when the time came to speak, it, the speech, would not make sense, could not make sense. Who would have thought that they would be transposed through those programs. Who could have imagined this?

The process, as best as he could figure, and of course what else could he do, the only thing he wouldn't do is to write it down, they couldn't make him, there couldn't be anything in it for him; the process is this. First you die. Then someone in Berkeley determines whether or not you are sufficiently important. Then that same person finds all the available text on you. Then a whole bunch of persons enter your data into the base. They seem to add some sort of A.I. program that then brings you back. When you first arrive however you must be brought up to date. For Foucault, this was a matter of a few days of data. Nietzsche and Spinoza, being further down the data stream, take longer. For Nietzsche, it took years; Spinoza, obviously, decades. And Spinoza is so much bigger than the others.[15] Now all of them were writing like fiends instead of just taking it easy. Why couldn't they just take it easy, he wondered. So, he walks into the room, sees that "mazel" is not available for a chat; looks around for Nietzsche, although he almost hopes he is *not* there. He is.

"Ah Michel," Nietzsche says familiarly, "I've been waiting for you. How awful of me not to recognize you through your work last night. Is all forgiven? Yes?" Foucault nods grimly. He lights a cigarette. Nietzsche looks pained. "How can this bother you?" Foucault asks indicating the cigarette. Nietzsche says nothing. Instead, he addresses the issue from the day before, "We were speaking of love? No?" Foucault says quickly, "Yes." "Well," says Nietzsche, "why don't you teach me what you know about it, you know more than I do." Foucault laughs.

Nietzsche feels in a confessional mode. He is overstimulated. He likes what he has done with Foucault. He feels as if this has been very good for him. He wants to tell Foucault how much this has meant to him; how much it has taught him; how good it has felt; how much pleasure he has experienced; how much he has learned about power. Alas, he does not know the etiquette. He does not know what the manly thing would be. So he is silent. But he is in a decidedly confessional mode. This is strange, this act, this series of acts, it erases the other power, the paradigmatic power I had since I have structured all his work. I am powerless in the face of this other strength he has. Imagine if he had channeled that strength to his real work. As Nietzsche thinks this he feels as if he has betrayed both himself and his work. Both Foucault and his work. Oh, he wishes he could speak with Foucault; he wishes he could confess.

Foucault is thinking that it is too bad that he cannot know what Nietzsche is thinking. He is not sure of the process yet. Maybe in a year the programmers will give them the contents of each others new thoughts. He sincerely hopes not. This will be too much. He is angry at the programmers. They have given this fake life. He couldn't help think, as he has thought each time he has performed since the, what?, new life, that the act is not real, that perhaps someone is recording it and will disseminate it, awful thought, scandalous invasion. But he would rather not just know Nietzsche's thoughts. He wants Nietzsche himself to share with him as he has shared with Nietzsche. Why the continuous undervaluation of sex? Why the immediate willingness for Nietzsche to say that Irigaray (Luce he called her, her not even dead) loved him and the thrice mediated impossibility of saying that Foucault has just loved Nietzsche? And hasn't he? Hasn't he?

It has been said of me, Foucault thinks, that "he has never had any problem concerning the links between science and literature, or the imaginary and the scientific, or the known and the lived, because the conception of knowledge impregnated and mobilized every threshold by making each one into the variable of the stratum which stood as a historical formation" (Deleuze 1986, pp. 51–52). And this is accurate, he thinks now. I did not just fill in details. But no one can see what I have done because they are focussed on my non-philosophical stance. Nietzsche that frenzied Nietzsche, that Dionysian enthusiast still fills the philosopher's subject position. The same person who would make of Nietzsche a philosopher with the same, how shall we say, stature as Spinoza, that GOD, writes of us all: "Nietzsche understood, having lived it himself, what constitutes the mystery of a philosopher's life. The philosopher appropriates the acetic virtues—humility, poverty, chastity—and makes them serve ends completely his own, extraordinary ends that are not very ascetic at all, in fact" (Deleuze 1988, p. 3). It is about us all because it says: Nietzsche *lived* without living; Spinoza *lived* without living, and, philosophers are so smart that they can do this thing. But those other rogues, those Foucauldian-types, those philosophers who follow Foucault are not content with understanding that humility, poverty, chastity—the philosophical virtues—can be transformed into power through thought rather than obedience. No, Foucault and Foucauldians break on through. Subsequently, they are those detail boys, the one who fill in the architectonic, handmaidens to the thinkers of thoughts of thoughts.

Foucault has worked himself up. He is ready to go another round with Nietzsche. Nietzsche does not say no.

Foucault will not reply when Nietzsche asks him, shortly after spectacular body work, if he knew or has known Deleuze. He has the upper hand; Nietzsche has just confessed that he likes, very much he said, the masks, and the cuffs. He says this shyly. Well good, Foucault thinks, but he says nothing. He is jealous of this new question. He need not reply and he does not. He almost mentions Lou and her whip but decides such cruelty serves no purpose. He *likes* Nietzsche after all. Nietzsche continues, he really has no sense of etiquette Foucault decides. He continues by saying, "I find it so amusing that at such provocative points he uses the

wrong name. It is charming." "For instance," Foucault says
tersely. He is angry. Nietzsche does not notice the pique. He
says, "Oh for example in the book on me he starts the section
on the body with the word 'Spinoza.' Is that not provocative?"
Foucault hates this talk, "Are we not men?" he says and
Nietzsche doesn't get it. "Well, yes," he says.

Foucault calls up the passage from his data bank. He
had not remembered the passage but indeed it reads: "Spinoza suggested a new direction for the sciences and philosophy. He said that we do not even know what a body *can
do*, we talk about consciousness and spirit and chatter on
about it all, but we do not know what a body is capable of,
what forces belong to it or what they are preparing for"
(Deleuze 1983, p. 39). Foucault's anger is elided momentarily by the thought that Nietzsche is contemplating his
skill with awe and respect. Then the bete noire of his life
returns: the old goat wants "mazel". See if I care, he thinks.
See if I care.[16]

The fear is used up, reopened and exposed as a fear
always already done away with. Whatever body is created by
an electronic net was already there for those in the think via
the Spinozist web of caring.[17]

4. Impediment to Political Action: Fear[18]

If we are using up fear in venues that introduce new
fears and paranoias, then we are using up all of our time in
places and strategies that remain at one level: the level of
information and more information. The death of metaphysics is supposed to have made the information work. The
politics of discourse, politics. And yet, on the eve of economy,
our feet in the world are not walking. They are approximat-
ing the same. How can we get a fear to overcome, that when
it is overcome will be at some more significant level: the level
of earth body politics. I think that the clue is in writing. In
turning every action self-conscious through its assimilation

to graphematic structure. If we can write through our fear and share it and write the old fear with our bodies, then the text and the body, the textual bodies, are necessarily in the world, but the writing has to be beyond sovereignty. What will we become beyond sovereignty?

Chapter Three

WRITING

1. Writing through to Fiction

Critical theory has as one of its conclusions, feminism. Feminism has as one of its conclusions, gender theory. Gender theory has as one of its conclusions, queer theory. There are, consequently, inherent reaction formations in the various academic disciplines against critical theory, feminism, gender theory, and queer theory. Fiction is writing that says on occasion what theory cannot say. Theory is writing that says on occasion what fiction cannot say. Kathy Acker goes beyond both with android fiction: fiction that theorizes the minds of people who one might meet on the net.[1] Acker takes all of this and comes up with theory for cyborgs: theory that makes real those who sense their artificiality.

Kathy Acker writes about sex. She also writes about gender and gender possibilities. Since her earliest writing, she has shaken up our assumptions about subjectivity and personal identity. Her techniques of using several genres, of filling in silent characters or historical figures from "other" material, or telling us the private actions and fantasies of other author's creations, exact an exciting glissage of personalities for the reader to reconstruct or simply enjoy. Her *In Memoriam to Identity* finishes what she started two decades earlier: the self, even the fictional self, is dissolved into the many aspects that a purported identity can take through perceptions, mis-perceptions and analyses. She gives us a complete dispersal of the self that is not phenomenologically dissonant with our experience. She describes alienation without alienating her readers. The self dispersal takes place against a backdrop where the characters understand, and the narrator(s) force the reader to understand, that politics are hopelessly corrupt, cities are bankrupt both morally and financially, and we have everything to fear for our sanity and survival. Why then, when one reads Kathy Acker, does one feel renewed, hopeful, re-connected with that which the works "tells" one that one cannot renew, cannot hope for, cannot connect with?[2] The answer, I suggest, lies in her ability to free one, even if only momentarily, from rigid ethical place settings. She gives permission to experience a radical freedom. In *Kathy Goes to Haiti*, for example, one is at first horrified that the title character seems unconcerned with the politics of the title country. But as one continues reading one is struck with *life*. She is concerned to love and to understand.[3]

In Memoriam to Identity is full of characters who assent to a rather pessimistic view of political reality. The reason I will continue to maintain that Acker's work is ultimately rejuvenating, hopeful, even *social* is tripart.[4] First, the anarchist force of Acker's work does not stem from a solitary or even from a very theoretical anarchism. The very dissolving of the ego seems to make group anarchy, and hence group loving and caring, possible. Second, Acker's brand of feminism (her love of women and womanly things) finishes off systemic philosophy and phallocentric discourse where it had to occur: outside of the academy. Finally, Acker plays a therapeutic role for her readers by articulating the tension we feel when, in the academy, we are confronted with our dual role of deconstructionist and erector of the same object: systemic thought. Anarchy is never far from these issues. It won't let itself disappear.[5]

2. Anarchy in the UK/USA

Co-optation happens before a lyric can be sung out. The anarchic force of punk and post-punk music seemed to dis-

appear during an observable duration. Despite the whim-
pering about Megadeth's cover of the old Sex Pistol's tune,
Dave Mustaine's anarchy is no more a sell-out than that of
Sid Vicious' before him—although we might argue that Mal-
colm McLaren's co-optation of all of them is more culpable
than that of the performers could be. But what possible force
can this term "co-optable" have in this discussion? When the
aim is to be co-opted, and when the results of being co-opted
are so magnificent, who will not clamor for such a co-optation. If and when we criticize Mustaine and not Vicious, Ellis
but not Acker, however, we do so only because we give priority to some sort of authorial status that we have no
justification for doing. The terms of "discoursing" have
changed radically. To be heard, one must already be in a
group network, a social or political network. The individual
intellectual is henceforth a fiction. Thus, charges of co-optation must be immensely specific to be meaningful. If and
when we criticize McLaren or City Lights or Combat Records or Warner Brothers, we do so only because we credit
the direction, the organization with more sophistication and
power than it *could* have. That is, we are antecedently valuing things for no reason but custom or ethical place setting.
This shows how far we are from anarchist thought when we
function as critics. "Anarchy was turned into mere fashion,
it seemed, before we could get our hands on it," or "Anarchy
as a potentially subversive force died in the street before it
could do anything" say armchair critics. But anarchy is lived
on the streets daily. It just doesn't always find its way into
the places that "we" look; the places that "we" are allowed to
notice. What I am pointing toward here, is over simplified
but the point under consideration is that in criticizing so-
called sell-outs in pop-culture, we are really buying into a
sort of holiness for pop-culture that is bizarre. It makes no
sense to attach "cultural" value to that which is a-cultural.
There cannot be something, in this day and age, that is not
a "sell-out" if we are seeing it.[6]

In academe, subversive strategies function as anarchy
in recent pop-culture. They arrive on the scene and are seemingly institutionalized before anything "real" "happens".

Foucault, in a middle period interview, talks about how surprised professors were to find that after they taught their students how oppressive the academic system was, the students did not oblige by joining rank with them; instead, they turned this knowledge against the professors who were, after all, part of the system under critique (Foucault 1989, pp. 67–68). Likewise, some academics who focus on street culture, are surprised to find that they are not a part of street culture just because they "know" about its representation in mass (mall?) culture. There is a paradox brought on by the leveling effect of a mass culture. On the one hand, we have an increasingly lower class professorate (Foucault 1989, p. 67) and an increasingly "low-brow" intellectual arena (Foucault 1990, pp. 44–45). On the other hand, we have an internal academic need to valorize the "low-brow" with "high-brow" theories. Some of the unintentionally hilarious work on rap and Madonna are good examples.[7] The paradox is in wanting it both ways. Academe wants to be down and dirty but to continue a pristine reign. Subversive (or transgressive) strategies are not likely to come out of this paradox.

Acker succeeds in being a vibrant voice, a critic, and maintaining an anarchic force, in part, because she makes all criticism internal to the creative process. She doesn't say: this is good anarchy, this is bad anarchy, according to some elaborate theoretical schema or anti-schema. She just wrote qua anarchist. This is such a simple point; still, it is easier described than performed. Hakim Bey, who advocates an extra-systemic anarchism, says that given the disappearance of the social, a new anarchist question has arisen. He says:

> When the Theorists speak of the disappearance of the Social they mean in part the impossibility of the "Social Revolution," and in part the impossibility of "the State"—the abyss of power, the end of the discourse of power. The anarchist question in this case should then be: Why *bother* to confront "power" which has lost all meaning, and become sheer Simulation? (Bey 1985, p. 128).[8]

Acker is working through this same question in her novel *In Memoriam to Identity*. How can we confront "love" when love cannot mean anything? How can we find ourselves, when we don't exist? How can we see the power such that we might directly confront it? What we should do is not something that can or ought to be precisely formulated in every case. Street problems cannot have academic answers. However, we do love, create ourselves and confront power. These facts count. The writing articulates love, self-creation and power; in so doing, it helps to find ways of effecting the disappearance of power. The writing gives voice to all the voices that power has papered over. By giving voice to the women of the Faulkner novels (particularly Caddy and Quentin from *The Sound and the Fury* and from *The Wild Palms*) we learn that the patriarchal voice is not all determining. That it determined Mrs. Compton, and the results of this we see in the Faulkner novels, themselves, does not mean that it determines all possible power and sentiment. *The Sound and the Fury* writes over love, creativity and power; Acker proves that it cannot erase love, creativity and power—even for fictional characters. Quentin-female does not disappear when she climbs down that tree with all of Jason's money. Quentin-male does disappear, literally from space and time. Quentin-female makes a life, survives, gives us hope. She does not find herself encased in the either/or of get a job, or don't get a job. She is an anarchic force and she is given, or she is, life. Even though that life is a frightening one, it is not determined through the old loves, the old powers, the old identities. Bey theorizes what Acker shows:

> Refusal of *Work* can take the forms of absenteeism, on-job drunkenness, sabotage, and sheer inattention—but it can also give rise to new modes of rebellion: more self-employment, participation in "black" economy and "lavoro nero," welfare scams and other criminal options, pot farming, etc.,—all more or less "invisible" activities compared to traditional leftist confrontational tactics such as the general strike (Bey 1985, p. 129).

Acker, I think, would agree that the leftist confrontational tactics or the commitment to Work are not our only options. We can refuse to participate in Work. Acker, however, shows the great risk of this choice: Airplane's sex work, for instance, is something that she must do to keep her free enough to work on her artistic endeavors, but something which she is constantly working to get away from so that she can be "real" again. This is an instance where anarchism meets feminism/gender theory (as Acker's work with Rimbaud shows). Participation in extra-systemic modes of survival are causally related in a systemic manner to the exploitation of persons who express gender freedom/sex freedom. To write (to perform, to understand selves) one must be extra-systemic to some degree. Another way to put this, is that the sort of writing that is power has to operate in an anti-raw power manner.

A final comparison with Bey's anarchy. Bey stresses the importance of joy and anti-authoritarianism to finding an anarchist life worth living:

> As Nietzsche said, if the world *could* come to an end, logically it would have done so; it has not, so it *does* not. And so, as one of the sufis said, no matter how many draughts of forbidden wine we drink, we will carry this raging thirst into eternity (Bey 1985, p. 128).

Acker also articulates this endless desire and life that will not allow us to completely dissolve. This desire and life is why I think that her works end up being so loving and nurturing. Reading Acker works better than therapy: because it is in fact full of the need to care and be cared for. Then after showing the need, it exhibits that need as possibility. Writing Acker, that is, reading Acker then writing, surely must be a political act.[9]

If Caddy and Quentin-female remain at the edge of dissolution with no new voice coming forth nothing happens. We are in death. Acker gives them voice through Capitol and Airplane. (It would be nice to have Dilsey have a voice too.

Her epitaph: They endured (William Faulkner 1929, p. 424). It makes a certain sense that Mrs. Compton isn't given a voice but the absence of Dilsey's voice remains problematic.) Capitol says this in the Acker novel:

> Will you be my daddy? I wanted to say. No one can tell me what to do. Sometimes I'm in ecstasy and I want to fuck every man in town and I don't care what the face is on the body I'm fucking. That's not evil it's ecstasy.
>
> During the day, Quentin and I walked down to where the swans were. Here I felt peaceful. I hadn't seen them because, for a long time, it had been winter. I had been scared they died in the cold and I couldn't bear when living things die. It's the helplessness, but I don't know whose helplessness (Acker 1990, p. 160).

The passage exemplifies the lack of situatedness for helplessness but the reaffirmation of life is present. It is interesting, but maybe not surprising, that both Bey and Acker are explicit in their disavowal of intellectual property. Bey's book has an anti-copyright. Acker says at the end of *In Memoriam to Identity*: "All the preceding has been taken from the poems of Arthur Rimbaud, the novels of William Faulkner, and biographical texts on Arthur Rimbaud and William Faulkner" (Acker 1990, p. 265).

3. Alternate Sexualities; Living

Acker's sexualism, her feminism, is a powerful antidote to the discourse the academy cannot kill. In some of its incarnations, feminism is an alternate sexuality. When it is not, one could argue, it replicates patriarchy. I know that at first this seems exclusive. But I believe that if we can be exclusive in feminism this is where it has to occur. If feminism does not force increased and diverse sexualities, it represses in identical ways to patriarchy. Feminism, in part, reclaims sexuality for all those who have been denied access to it. Or, more precisely, lifts the prohibition towards life. In still other words, feminism becomes gender anarchy. If one is not allowed to use one's body for the pleasure that one seeks, then one cannot be really said to be living. Granted, some feminisms have restricted sexuality and sexualities. I have tried to affirm that "Not wanting to shut anyone down for their explorations into what is available to them as possibilities, I won't say that such feminists are wrong." But I cannot. I do think that feminism is most productive and liberating when it helps us learn to articulate and recognize desire and to distinguish desire from learned responses masquerading as desire and which thereby disempower those who feel it or fail to feel it.[10] That feminisms can be identical to alternate sexualities is crucial, I think, to understanding Acker's feminisms. Her appropriation of Rimbaud's homosexuality is a crucial feminist step. It is Rimbaud, in *In Memoriam to Identity* who intimates:

> Just like the sexual—the architectural and philosophical systems of the city collapsed between five and ten years ago. This collapse of reason rather than theism—this collapse of absolutism—these collapsed bridges are linking the city's concrete chaos to the hills outside the city. In this fantastic landscape, feminism is being born (Acker 1990, p. 68).

Feminism does not arise out of the dissolution of the religious self. On the contrary, feminism arises when the arguments, the ratiocinations fail to convince anyone, even their practioneers. Feminism is on the outskirts of town, slowly crossing the collapsed bridges to reinstate life and desire. When the arguments failed, it was as if, as Wittgenstein says and Descartes before him also said, "all is plunged into extricable darkness." But this darkness is our hope, the ability for rebirth and rejuvenation. It is here that we can reclaim our childhood and start over again as alive. (Remember Capitol: Will you be my daddy?) Rimbaud is given lines about childhood as well. He says that childhood is one place where freedom (life) is found and that the distillation of childhood is a kind of language we should not forget. His words are feminist a la Irigaray. She argues that it is through new kinds of articulation that we will uncover our lost origins.[11] Rimbaud says:

> Language is alive in the land of childhood. Since language and the flesh are not separate here, language being real, every vowel has a color. A is black; E is white; I, red; O, blue; U, green. The form and direction of each vowel is instinctive rhythm. Language is truly myth. All my senses touch words. Words touch the senses. Language isn't only translation, for the word is blood.
> At first this is all just theoretical (Acker, pp. 89–90).

Theory is first but it is not last. Even in something as basic as language. Anarchy is also something basic. And it cannot find its form in theory. What is less clear is whether or not it could be found in the places that are devoted to theory. Can we do what needs to be done from the academy? This is the question to which I turn. Before doing so, I remind my readers, that I have already committed myself to asserting that the solutions to many personal and social problems are to be found in writing. So in asking this question, it is really specifically about academe.

4. We Need Language(s) for Analysis

Writing is increasingly conscious of itself as therapeutic philosophy. Acker serves as analyst for schizo-times. She forces us to do analysis of self—to search for the pre-linguistic time of a purity we long for. Can that purity exist in academe? One would think that it is especially here that it could be found. After all, is this not the reason for the academy's first existence? One cannot think well when one is troubled by matters of survival. One can only think well when the matters of survival are already attended to for one. But, so much has changed. For one thing, universities are those strange things now that continue with the myth of such pursuit of pure truth (variously named, even as post-modernism—yes!) but also the training ground for literal survival. What is the first purity?

> Here, the country of childhood no longer hurt, for the country of marriage no longer existed. Here, at the border, in the midst of the *puddles* released by the torrents of that month, women found the fish they wanted to serve for dinner. When fish smell too much, they're definitely dead.
> If childhood had been the season for sickness, these fish, these scales of fingernails, heralded the body of health. The religious body. Blood, touch of flesh, name here the sacred personages and holy Vestals: hair, eyes, lips, cheeks, bones, muscles, mucous tissues, organs that smell when dead when alive, garbage caught inside the living, marrow, air, water, limbs caught at their upper ends to the torso, ligaments. Name that Virgin Who sustains me in the middle of my heart, *Purity*, Who overflows into this river of blood, these emotions. All her emotions and secretions are holy. Perhaps even a certain murder. Sustain this dream (Acker 1990, p. 65).

My guess is that her writing is necessary to her. She is one of the rare writers whose writings become personal and necessary to her readers. (Nietzsche is another such voice.) What can we learn from her without theorizing her out of her relevance? Or, can we do theory, criticism, without being merely vampirish? If Acker is what I say she is, why not just *read* her? How do we find the other side of voice/fiction/theory? What matter finally is analysis? The writing and the reading as analysis-schizoanalysis.

5. Academic Tension: Re-writing

It is something that we struggle with as academics. What can we say and what can we write? What are we allowed? What can we allow ourselves? We have increasingly pushed this mostly subliminal discourse to the front and it is embarrassing. At least I am embarrassed that universities have policies denying faculty and students the right (right?) to sleep with each other. At least I am embarrassed that universities have strict distinctions between "teaching" "research" and "service!" Make no mistake, such liaisons are almost certainly bad for everyone involved. Make no mistake, we need our procedures! Many things that are bad for everyone involved, we would agree, should not be proscribed. Why do we think that talking about something requires an end result in the form of a policy? We do. Why do we toss and turn over what we have said in class? We do. Why do we worry about the lines we write? We do. Studies have been conducted. Much of what we write is not read. This is something most of us know. So, why do we worry about the lines we write? We do. Increasingly there is something very much in bad faith about attaching oneself to an institution. It is true that we can formulate important policy from those positions. It is also true that we are contaminated. We are.

Siegle characterizes Acker's work like this:

> Although cultural conservatives might feel a bit uncomfortable with the assertion, there is nonetheless something to the claim that Acker is almost sacramental in her approach to individuality and to the world, that her ends are profoundly therapeutic, that her values are radically demystified forms of mythologized metaphors become Megalons, and that her practice of fiction is an attempt to regain for narrative a voice and form that are commensurate with our information age but capable of performing, against that age's colonization of its "processors," the novel's quite traditional function of renewing the possibility for fresh subjectivity (Siegle 1989, p. 101).

This is a description of what we should and can do when we are educating—whether as friends, professors, students, lovers. We should write and re-write ourselves in front of those with whom we have connections until they are able to appreciate that they are capable of adopting fresh subjectivities. When we fail to do this, our failure is guilty. We should let people rewrite themselves in front of us with safe conditions.

A consequence of this is that if we truly desire the space in which to be, then we should abandon liberalism and its attendant electoral strategies for the same reason and in the same way that many feminists have already abandoned phallocentric discourse. Phallocentric discourse cannot *just* be abandoned because there it is over and against us. Still, by becoming increasingly aware of the potency and impotency of that discourse, many of us believe that we can fight it more effectively or develop new voices or discourses external to it or repeat its resisting strategies subversively. So we abandon this discourse by refusing total assimilation to it. We should similarly abandon liberalism. Its discourses cannot yield strategies which adequately represent the selves we might become.

The climate for writing has reached new lows; it forces us toward communal strategies that transcend the differences of the diverse feminisms and other subject positions. Because I believe that we are in crisis, this theme will be discussed in largely practical terms. I use "communal" to qualify groups or strategies formed or endorsed by real communities. For me, real communities always form and work within civil society and are always opposed to state or polity. Groups that appear to be communities, that is, groups that appear marginalized, that ostensibly share interests, or that seem to have some grounding, but that also have as one of their properties that their words or actions support the state, are not actually communities. Such groups cannot be legitimated because they derive their interests from state interests and, I believe, states cannot be legitimated. My suggestion for a practical strategy, that we abandon liberalism (in theory, in practice, really abandon it), solidifies our discourse and practice outside of state power.

Still, we need the language for analysis; the language that will allow us to write outside the academy from within. That language will be the result of a communal effort—an effort of thought thinking itself as the writing of oneself as other.

Chapter Four

FROM PAPER VILLAGE
TO VIRTUAL COMMUNITY

... because they spent their lives exploring meaning—the meaning of words, of symptoms, of dreams, of texts, of crimes, of darkness with or without end—their deaths are open to interpretation. Whether challenging, absurd or stupid, their deaths are part of the meaning they constructed. Death lends drama to their work, but also, paradoxically, cancels it out, with the nonchalance of a Stoic suicide.[1]

1. Kierkegaard's Paper Village

Once upon a time a man wrote a series of characters through which he proceeded to live. This living, this part of living, was fairly unproblematic. Presumably there were many complex reasons for writing in this way. He must have made decisions, maybe not the big one, the decision not to "own" his own words; still, he must have made countless decisions about the authorship that transcend by leaps and bounds, the cliche is necessary, here, now, that transcend the explanations he gives at the end of *Concluding Unscientific Postscript*.

I can imagine him thinking about the sorts of names to give the characters through whom he writes. I can picture him, in his ill-fitting pants, his bad haircuts, his angry/kind face showing delight when he lights upon just the right name: Victor Eremita. Yes! That is it. I can see his eyes, sleeping now, twitching with dreams he will not remember, but which will work their way into his books as if by magic. These details, surely false, surely fictive, are details that couch and cloud the authorship. Soren mentioning to a friend (a friend!) that he is unable to attend dinner because ... Johannes hiding, holding his breath, keeping curtains drawn because Soren really is not "at home."

Soren is not really at home but does Soren "talk to" Johannes? Does he make small talk or do they jump right in to existential matters? Probably these questions of mine are precisely the wrong ones. These questions presuppose at best sickness and at worst dishonesty as properties of the authorship. And as presuppositions go these are too judgmental, too false. But where is the community that says: be honest when you write? Where is the group of persons who presuppose that one should find the truth about the selves who inhabit one; that one ought to spill them all over. Find an excess. Writing to and from—the voice within us? the ears without? Are all paper villages villages of one? Eremita meet Climacus! Keeping them straight must have been a chore in every sense and on every level. Kierkegaard is exhausted by the effort. He tries to write each one separately: he works hard at not letting them enter into conversations with each other. An author yields a book. Did the author take the *work* to create the other author or was that nothing, just another fact to work with? Was getting the work out the hard part? There is an intimacy to the writing. One hears and reads "Soren." One writes and says "Soren." I do not hear "Rene" nor "Martin." Sometimes "Friedrich" but as disrespect. Why are we allowed "Soren?"

Enter the reader. The reader comes warily. Is the space of Kierkegaardian discourse hermetically sealed? How can the reader enter that communication? How can the village be expanded to include more than those already there by authorial intent? Is a reader of the authorship always voyeuristic? Never a true participant? Do we say "Soren" because there is something familial, something familiar here, something intimate? Do we wish we were friends with him? Can we decide to let Kierkegaard go? To let him be? The reader is at liberty to go, at liberty to refuse the texts, to leave. Still, certain texts and certain authorities bind you to their villages whether you refuse them or not. Ignorance of the law is no defense. The Kantian imperative binds because we know it even if we don't know it in its particulars.

Can community be a series of oneway streets? Individuals thinking similar thoughts with no in-between? That is, individuals in parallel lines, identical in their re-thinking and thinking? No space for negotiation? What if one read a text and felt as if every word written there were one's own? As if it were not written by an anterior and exterior other but by one's voice at some other time, in some other place? What is Kierkegaard trying to tell us by fragmenting himself? Is he saying that there is no consensus and that this is a good thing? That dissent, negation, flow, deterritorilization, unnamedness, difference, that these are the only things? Does each of Kierkegaard's author's have intentions of their own? Who is he? Who are they? What is their ontological status? Are they real? Could Russell help us here? Really? Does he, do *they*, care about how (t)he(y) is(are) understood? Is he merely expressing himself? Is there an injustice done here by using the term "merely" as I have done? To whom is this injustice done, if indeed it is done? Does Kierkegaard care if he is understood? What would it take to understand him?

Kierkegaard himself writes in his doctoral dissertation on the concept of irony (of course) that Socrates

> brought the individual under the force of his dialectical vacuum pump, deprived him of the atmospheric air in which he was accustomed to breathe, and abandoned him. For such individuals everything was now lost, except insofar as they were able to breathe in an ether. Yet Socrates no longer concerned himself with them, but hastened to new experiments (Kierkegaard 1965, p. 203).[2]

Socrates talking to his friends in the woods or in the open spaces. Socrates bringing them into a dialectical nothingness, bringing them to the meaning that what they had had, the meager knowledge that got them through their days, was *nothing*. What you need, Kierkegaard's Socrates seems to be saying, is to come *up* here with me. Quickly, they would see that not only was he right, that their knowledge was no knowledge, but also, that they could not be *him*, could not perform this thinking thing. Could not even function parallel to him. And then he abandons them. If Kierkegaard is right, then of course he abandoned them. He would have had no choice. To go further with them would be to overstep his bounds, would be to bind them to him in ways that would assure their not acquiring the ether-lung. Benign neglect. Merciful separation. Midwife of men. It is not as if any transition from dependence to independence is easy.

Kierkegaard writes Victor Eremita who finds a diary that is written by Joannes about Cordelia. It is Eremita who tells the story, who pilfers the diary of the seducer. Who exposes this private document—this exposure hidden by *layers* of authors. Who is not the seducer but who seduces somehow. When Victor Eremita tries to introduce us to the seducer, whose (dreary) diary we are about to read, Eremita describes the seducer's poetic temperament" as "not rich enough, or, perhaps, not poor enough to distinguish poetry and reality from one another. The poetical was the *more* he himself brought with him. This *more* was the poetical he enjoyed in the poetic situation of reality (Eremita 1959, p. 301). The seducer is a playful sort of fellow. He wants to see what will happen if he does this seducing thing. What will happen if he does nothing? He is playful and petty. Socrates, like the seducer, cannot stop playing with people. He gets them interested, gets their blood going, piques them diagonally—then, drops them. The seducer is an inferior copy of this. He does not drop the seduced so that she can flourish, does not give her her independence for her, no, he drops her after seducing her successfully, so that *he* can flourish and so that *he* can be independent. He is a man who is patterned after Socrates who is patterned after a sort of a . . . god. She is a woman. She is a woman who is not patterned after Socrates who is not patterned after a sort of . . . god. The seducer considers giving her philosophy when he opines that "if I were a god, I would do for her what Neptune did for a nymph: I would change her into a man" (Eremita 1944, p. 440). Maybe if she were a man and he were still who he is when he was in love with her, then he could talk to her and get her to a point where he could abandon her *meaningfully* for both of them.

This paper village is so crowded. It makes me so claustrophobic. Every relation telling us that we are responsible for interpreting every relation. Socrates tells Kierkegaard, through his clever use of irony which does not pervert itself over the centuries and through the seas, that while his interlocutors do not attain his heights, Kierkegaard can. Kierkegaard responds through his worshipful, yet manly, discussion of the midwife, that he would talk with him, if they were both there in the same space. It is so cozy how they could abandon each other manfully in full fellowship and community. The seducer, Johannes, writing damp letters to Cordelia, the seduced, making a paper bond, a paper chain, to be pulled apart as the lesson, the lesson that there is only one love, one God. And that that love, that God is not interested in sentiment. This paper village. Everyone talking and no one listening.

Writing letters. Reading philosophy as if letters to oneself. Is that wrong? Kierkegaard looking for the private meaning that Socrates offers him through Plato. Is that a peculiar way to read? Is it wrong? Do we write each other letters when we write philosophy? Is writing itself the same as philosophy? Is every attempt at filling up a page with signifiers an attempt at settling down some meanings, giving ourselves an anchor? What makes philosophical writing philosophy? What makes a sovereign communication sovereign? Deleuze and Guattari are quite clear on one point: communication is not the same as philosophy. Philosophy is something altogether different.[3]

2. *Cixous Writing Herself to Herself For Herself In Herself*

This title gives the wrong impression. She writes herself to herself for herself in herself but is not in the least narcissistic. Using the title would imply that perhaps she, no more than Kierkegaard's Socrates, no more than Kierkegaard's Eremita's Seducer, cares for the other, the anterior or exterior other. But she does and she does by writing herself to herself for herself in herself.

According to Cixous, "to begin (writing, living) we must have death" (Cixous 1993, p. 7). To understand our relation to the dead we must rethink "what is your death and my death, which are inseparable. Writing originates in this relationship" (Cixous 1993, pp. 12–13). Writing originates in the knowledge that we are alike in our deaths, in our being-toward-death. We are already in a village. Together. Joined by death. What does this presuppose? What does this promise for community?

"My voice," Cixous writes "repels death; my death; your death; my voice is my other. I write and you are not dead. The other is safe if I write" (Cixous 1991, p. 4). Cixous fragmenting herself *as* herself makes a step beyond Kierkegaard. Is this a baby step or a giant step? Mother, may I? May I ask what is this staving off of death? Why do we strive to find ourselves in our deaths only to deny it? "Writing is God" (Cixous 1991, p. 11).[4] Well, God creates and in that sense writing is God, the reader can play with this image, with this power. Cixous calls us up short: "But it is not your God" (Cixous 1991, p. 11). It is not your God. My voice is my other god is repelling death is what is the case about the world.

For Cixous, my voice is my other and that other, that voice repels death. There is necessarily something else. To write, one must write from somewhere. One must find a place from which there is something to write. *My voice is my other*. "One cannot be one's own source" (Cixous 1991, p. 43). The author is in truth for herself. She writes beautifully. She writes beautiful titles. "The Author in Truth." She says, writing,

> Explain the inexplicable. However, it is true that what is most true goes like this: either you know without knowing, and this unknowing knowledge is a flash of joy the other shares with you, or else there is nothing. You'll never convert someone who is not already converted. You'll never touch a heart planted on another planet (Cixous 1991, p. 158).

Either there is ignorant knowledge or there is nothing. Either one already knew the extent to which one could not know or that knowledge cannot be brought to light, cannot be taught. Either you are on this planet or you are not, above ground or in the cave. How can there be a most true? Isn't it the case that what is true is what is present to me and that part of what is present to me is the flash we share? When we are lucky? In what sense is that flash more true than other flashes? That which accompanies silence before a storm? That which strikes Mickey Mouse's broom in Disney's Strauss's "The Sorcerer's Apprentice?"

Kierkegaard dissertates concerning Socrates and asserts that Socrates'

> . . . ignorance was the eternal triumph over the phenomenon, a triumph which neither a particular phenomenon nor the sum total of phenomena could wrest from him, but by virtue of which he triumphed at ever moment over the phenomenon. In this way he freed the individual from every commitment, freed him in the same why that he himself was free (Kierkegaard 1965, p. 200).

Well, which is it Kierkegaard? Is the individual freed or is the individual abandoned? Is everything forever lost for this individual? It seems quite clear that Kierkegaard is not equating freedom with everything being lost although he may well be equating freedom with being abandoned. Then the interesting relation would be that between freedom and being abandoned after having been shown some sort of path, some possible power over phenomenon. Freedom as the power to understand things that aren't really there? Explain the inexplicable. Irigaray does not "pussy-foot" around. She is able to say with her authority:

> Take back this horizon: mortal, and consider that Truth has always been a lying mask for your truth. Death's most terrible aspect lies in the charades you have invented to separate it from you. And from me (Irigaray 1992, p. 20).

3. Electronic Communities

Christopher Langton is maybe the only person in the world who has experienced life while observing (out of the corner of his eye!) cellular automata do their life thing. The story goes: he was working late in the computer lab when all of a sudden he *knew* that there was someone in the room with him. It turns out that what he felt was Conway's "life" running on a monitor just out of his sight. He had "felt" artificial "life." I like to think of him shrugging it off as some strange but unimportant event, but, him feeling a little bit spooky. I like to think of him laughing at the weirdness of it.

Once upon a time there was this guy Chris Langton. And he was sitting in this room just sort of not knowing if he should do this or that, when all of a sudden he was virtually certain that there was someone else in the room. There was. A life program. He sensed this "out of the corner of his eye."[5] What is the meaning of this story? There are days when this is my favorite story and I try to think of a good way to tell it. It is such an impossible story. So lovely and innocent and yet so anxiety producing.

So calming. To have been able to feel something like community, well, at least *presence* of something else, of something with intelligence, some other right there with one, and then to know with certainty that it was nothing of the sort, not even one's voice, even if one were to attenuate meaning to ridiculous lengths. Is this the story of paper villages?

Now Teddy Bears can meet each as each other's love objects quite readily. One can receive invitations to the Dead Artist Trailer Park that one can take seriously. One can fight with some unknown about the meaning of some small part of Deleuzian philosophy. No faces. No voices. But a deep rich tenor. Not all surface as some would have us believe.

Connections are easily made, but writing is sometimes too easy.[6] Pseudonyms are so quickly adopted and cast off that we are written before we have spoken or thought. To break through to our many selves and to others, we must keep some private paper for writing. It is the only safe thing to do.[7] Not just because there must be the allusion of private space. The main reason is that the power attendant on an immediately transparent public pretends an action that is not committed. The only safe thing is to do. And yet.

NOTES

Introduction

1. Derrida 1982, p. 17.

2. "The mind does not know itself, except as in so far as it perceives the ideas of the modifications of the body" (Spinoza 1955, II, XXIII).

3. One could write, for example, that on the one hand one is torn; on the other hand one is torn. That is to say one plans, one attempts to quit smoking. That is to say one loses faith in yet one more logically possible redemption. That is to say one is torn. One knows as a matter of record and document, that one is to plunge into oneself; it is apparent that one is beyond the objectivities and subjectivities that lose the essential oneness of the one in which one finds oneself. Nonetheless on the one hand one is torn; on the other hand one is torn. In other words, one does not find oneself; one does not know where to look.

One knows that one is more than one's roles and less than one's roles but still when one finds oneself outside of one's roles one is even more lost. It is summer. It is summer vacation. Although I am not completely student, I am not completely academic. Thus I have a false belief that I know to be a false belief in my consequent freedom—consequent to its being summer and my being partly student and partly academic. I have a sense of freedom that three months stand before me during which I have no earth shattering obligations, no assignments, no papers to either write or grade. But because I am only partly student, and because of the choice I have made with respect to my profession, already partly academic, I experience the urgent (but falsely urgent) need to produce a piece of work. I tell myself that the urgency is false because it follows from the hollowness of my academic necessities. But, foolish as always, I believe that the sense of urgency stems from the need to produce free work. I say, "I have three months of (falsely) perceived freedom during which I have no earth shattering obligations, no assignments, no papers to either write or grade."

The first week I drink myself senseless. I drink the kind of drunk that stupefies to the point that only in the hangover can I perceive myself as a body and I am so stupefied that my toxicity has a pleasant, numbing effect. I cover myself in numbness. Then, on the first day of the second week I find within myself the need for energy. I exercise vigorously for an hour and a half; I sweat out toxins; I reassemble the past semester's files; I take books back to the library; I plug in my telephone; I fulfill my social obligations; I begin, again, to cease merely to exist. I say, "I will do something. I will inflate this pointless life with meaning. I will produce a work because the profession I have chosen requires it. I am a conceptual proletarian."

One summer, thanks to no mistakes on my part, I ended up in Paris with a childhood friend with whom I hadn't any contact since my childhood. She was two years younger than me and much more energetic than I have ever been. Because the arrangement was in no way my fault I did nothing to even out our differences nor to accommodate her desires to do something. Cally is an active sort but mildly agoraphobic and would go nowhere alone. I did try on occasion to make things more bearable for her. For instance, I would sometimes walk the seven blocks it took to get to the Luxembourg Gardens. There we would sit until she got bored and would persuade me to rearrange myself and walk the seven blocks back to our rooms. I would write: Dear Mamma, Cally and I find much to amuse us. It is very pretty in the parks and yesterday [I would lie] we saw a very interesting film [here I would crib some review]. I miss everyone at home and look forward to the time when I will be with you again. Please let me know if you still plan to meet us here before you and Dad take your vacation. Love, Kelly.

. . . Yes. For two months, Kelly and Cally shared rooms—a truly cacophonous, though mostly silent, couple—Kelly and Cally, Kelly and Cally.

The two scenes which most stand out in my mind when I think about that summer vacation (then I was a complete student with summers truly off, no thought about works to be produced) are not remarkable. However, if memory serves, and it may well not, they are typical not only of that summer but of every summer the winters, springs and falls corresponding to which I was a complete student. I have had atypically seven such summers. Ah, there were more but they were attached to school years lived at home and the summer mornings were interrupted with calls to clean the toilet or help with lunch or see to my brothers' needs. I have many brothers and they still, coming home for some holiday, expect me and my sisters to see to their needs. This is remarkable to me. Seven summers away from home and school and with no brothers.

One scene I remember vividly could have occurred more than once in that very long two months. The months in Paris. Kelly and Cally. Kelly and Cally. We had two rooms—a fairly large sitting room and a bedroom. We had, in addition to these rooms, a kitchen, a bathroom and an entry way. I spent most of my time in one of the twin beds. Of course, I should note that this is what I remember. It may have been different. The wallpaper had a very nice texture although it was nothing to look at. It was always cool, even through the oppressive heat of that awful summer. I had been awake for some time and I was engaged in an analysis of my dream—the one I had just had. Now, it may be that one never dreams—that one merely makes stories up on waking and believes that one had lived this story while sleeping. But this morning I believed that I had lived this story while sleeping. I mean, I believed that I experienced the dream while I was asleep and not just as a false after-image. This morning I believed that I had dreamt, or, I had in fact dreamt, that I was eighteen years old. (At the time of this alleged dream, I was nearly seventeen years old.) Being eighteen I had decided to go swimming in the pool on the top deck of the S.S. France on which craft I had booked passage to, I think, New York. Arriving at the pool, after searching for some time the correct stairway, can you believe it? the correct stairway, I decided that on second thought everyone in the pool was much older than eighteen and in any case it could wait, I lay down on the side of the pool loving the feel of the warm concrete, a sensation I have loved since I was able to be pool-side, say, from the age of three, or maybe four. Quickly the sensation of warmth ceased to be absolutely pleasurable so I trailed my hand back and forth in the cool water.

I have a theory that people who develop sleep disorders do so on purpose. It's a well known fact that you must sleep a certain amount of hours in order to dream. It's a well known fact that people take anti-depressants so that they will sleep enough to dream so that they don't go crazy. It's a well known fact that sleep must be deep to hold a dream. People who can't sleep choose to avoid their dreams because they have a hatred of their dream selves who do such wicked things. Narcophobia is the theory I have. It's the agoraphobia of night-people.

That was the whole dream. The analysis of this transparent little dream did little for me except to remind me that it was, in reality, warm; subsequently, I began mechanically to lightly caress the cool and pleasantly textured wallpaper above my bed. This may have gone on for several minutes or for a significant percentage of an hour or for even longer. I ceased caressing the wall in this soothing manner when Cally said, "Kelly, you are so odd."

Such was our relationship and such was the nature in which we passed time. And, of course, I wanted Cally and I loved Cally and she wanted Kelly, me, and loved Kelly. But we were seventeen and we were friends, for Christ sake, and friends didn't. It didn't bear thinking. Or maybe this is what I remember.

Another scene I remember precisely, which is to say that when I think of it, my head is filled with a clear and distinct idea of it although it is likely that each occurrence of said clear and distinct idea is wildly (and widely) different from every other such occurrence, is the following. Cally has asked me if I would like to do something. (To her this meant going to a concert or to the theater but becoming interested on the way in something else exciting and unplanned.) One version of this scene is that we go to a performance of a Beckett play but on the way we meet a person who is interested in teaching us the mysteries of the Tarot. The other version is that we make it to the play. Both versions are accompanied by sensations of an oppressive heat, a heat that creases your eyelids into trillions of puffy layers, a heat that feels like a bad trip. We get on the metro at Odeon but we must change somewhere—a big station in which Ramses' remains (or facsimiles thereof) are on display.

Once we went on a tour of the sewers but I have no clear recollection of this. It is recorded in my diary: Cally cajoled me into circumambulating the catacombs of Paris. Not really. We went on a guided tour of the sewers. It was damp and smelly but not so hot there as it had been here. For this respite from the heat I would endure a second tour (guided!) of any city's sewer.

Cally had a metro map and three different tour guide books of Paris. She had a camera which she never once used. She was afraid that carrying it would make her look dweeb-like. She is carrying a purse and the guide books. It is very hot in the trolley-like car. I look down and see to my horror that I have made a pool of sweat on the floor. I am very young. I still believe that everyone is very interested in observing all of my body moves and functions. The horror subsides when I notice that every rider has a similar pool. I get an urge to giggle but this too passes. The people in the car are so hot and so close to hysteria that something in their sense of community keeps them from manifestations of hysteria: the giggle, the losing control, the panic-chicken and so on. Like me, they fear the real potential for a massive, insane outburst. The moment passes; we have regained our composure. Both versions of this clear and distinct memory (memory! idea!) contain the sweat scene. The memories diverge at Ramses' station. Cally, of course, would remember the name of the station.

In the aborted-attempt-at-seeing-the-Beckett-play version we run across a man named Patrick. He is Belgian. He asks us directions to a train station which hysterically—we find so much to be hysterical, it is so hot—turns out to be the one in which he stands just down two floors. Up two floors? Ask Cally. We laugh. Like idiots. We are young and turned on. Let's do it our laughter says. This is the play between Cally and Kelly. Patrick, of course, misinterprets, and who can blame him since Cally and Kelly misinterpret. We laugh. Like children. He is very tall and I find him insane. Cally finds him charming. He says "Well, here I am already." We say "Well, yes, there you are and you don't even have to look for where you were going." Lamely, we say "Coffee?" He finds our babyish, hysterical, laugh-talk amusing and says "Well, why don't I read your fortunes."

This is all helter, skelter, mechanically neat through the hysterical heat. I say "We are drained by Fall. We are mechanically neat." Cally rolls her eyes and then we are sitting in a stupid cafe and she is flirting with him and he is flirting with her and I am *de trop* but I don't mind. I listen to the idiotic things they say to each other and think how idiotic the things they are saying are and how much more clever I am and really I am better looking than Cally too. I get bored with the mating dance, for this is what it is, cards akimbo on the table top, serious people looking askance at us, people who are not serious thinking, well, how dull, the Tarot. So I say, hating myself for having this talk of mine come out like whine, like I cared that they were flirting back and forth like crazed tweety birds, I say, "Tell my fortune too."

In the second version (strange things these clear and distinct ideas which contradict each other) we arrive without incident at the play. The play is performed for an audience of tourists. Each player repeats each line three times: once in French, once in German, once in English. We are amused. Shortly after the performance we have, I think, a cup of coffee, or perhaps a soda; we return to our summer domicile. Cally broods; I sleep.

I have always been unable to keep a diary in winter, fall or spring. It is only in the summer that I write a diary. I read these diaries, sometimes, during the winter, fall or spring. Then, maybe because I am partly academic and partly student, or, maybe because I have been a student for so long, but, most likely because I am human, more on being human later, I analyze what I find written there. Summer is like a dream. It could be that summer is what we make up in the fall.

What I do (although not what I answer to the question, persistently posed by men who will not react with anything but "I am a man" if the question were asked of them—I have never had a woman ask me that question: "What do you do?") is to analyze my life with respect to other lives usually but not necessarily human ones. For instance, because I think more than I act (not out of sheer laziness but because the one thing I enjoy more than the other) I am not quite vegetarian. I am morally certain that to be vegetarian is the way to be. The compelling reasons are (1) I can survive healthily (and I know how to so survive) without consuming other animals and there is no justification for consuming them. Although (1) is not alone a sufficient reason for not eating flesh, it is necessary to that mode of being. (Mode of being!) (2) I can think of no justification to justify my killing an animal except for my survival or for the survival of some human in my presence. (3) When my best friend Lorenzo (Kelly and Lorenzo, Kelly and Lorenzo) and I go swimming at our favorite pond (it is clear, completely surrounded by dense forests in which one can distinguish, from other sounds, immense sounds of frogs and one can see crows, swallows and an occasional hawk) we float, when we tire of swimming, on rubber rafts. The day is long and hot; our skin is tight and warm, burning really, from the sun. We are so tired from swimming and from being so hot. Laying on rafts we trail our hands in the water. I am (neurotically) fearful of the fish which we can see if we create a shadow with our heads and hands. Lorenzo is not fearful of fish. His phobia is of sado-masochistic sex. But he is not afraid of fish. I know a woman who is afraid of fish because when she was very young her brother chased her around the house holding a sardine and making hideous boy-like noises, ssumprhr, hissssssssssmrprhrgph, arrrgggharagsssssmph. Lorenzo finds a school of fish and lowers his hand deep into the water—to his elbow at least. He does not move a muscle. Soon a fish will approach the hand eventually bumping into it with its nose. It examines this strange body which to it consists of a long white immobile appendage and a definitely inorganic slab of bright orange matter. Despite the strangeness of this big "animal" which confronts it, the fish tries to make a relationship with it. To eat it? Perhaps. But I have read that fish of this sort (trout, bass and large flat things that look like bloated, discolored goldfish) never eat anything bigger than themselves unless it (the other) is already dead. The reason is survival. Nevertheless, as you have seen my first reason (but only my first) for refraining from eating flesh has to do with survival. Do fish have other reasons about which we can know nothing? The only motive we can reasonably universalize (universalize?) to fish (or other animals) is survival. Do we do fish a disservice by propagating a fiction that their desires are so limited? Their ability to play so impossible? I swear to God, Lorenzo plays with fish. But they play back. I mean, of course, dogs do this. But FISH.

The third reason I do not consume flesh (but I *do*, if someone asks me to a party and there is no suitable vegetarian fare I will eat stuffed shrimp, I will eat swordfish glazed with orange sauce) is that the fish play with Lorenzo. They try to make him move or show some life. Are they sad by what looks like near death? Are they trying to cheer him up? The animal they see does not move but surely they sense the warmth. Do they want to revive it because they are Kantians and even though things like that kill them they have an obligation to. . . ? The fish's perspective is objectively limited. That is, we do know that it cannot know that Lorenzo's arm, so inert and helpless in the water, is structurally identical to the one which attached to a body on the shore is casting a reel. This same arm now, with the help of another, places a reel between two rocks so that the whole body can devote its energy to teaching its baby body to cast a reel of its own.

(4) The rain forests. (5) Chickens without beaks. (6) The intelligence of pigs. Nearby in the global village is a pig farm. Their (the pigs') favorite food is the stale doughnut. Their owner acquires the stale doughnut from a national outlet of fresh doughnuts. The product is fried in beef fat. One day the pigs, feeling like some doughnuts, break out of prison, trot directly to this shop, miles away, a place they have never been before. This, I suppose, could be explained by an analysis which reduces their motives to survival and their actions to instinct. So too can the French Revolution, for example. How unlikely an explanation! I imagine these pigs motivated by pure pleasure (they are in no danger of starvation and I presume that their owner is incapable of informing them that the plan is to kill and eat them—it is not from an executioner they flee.) (The French Revolution fits the survival model much more tightly.) Pleasure is not the only alternative motivation for these pigs; it is a plausible one. So any of us could go on about motivation here. And that is just the start of the whole thing in any case. Maybe they read maps that we can't see. It is enough anyway just to notice that there is no reason to eat flesh. Much less reason, in fact, than pigs have to break out of their prison to find doughnuts. On occasion, however, I eat fish or a snail. I love snails dripping a mild garlic butter sitting cutely in those darling little dishes. There is no reason for this callousness. Lorenzo eats meat of all kinds. He doesn't care about this issue. He says, "Kelly, be serious. You know I don't think that life is so long that each action has to be calculated in terms of its global consequences. You know, you know, if I thought you believed that there is no reason to eat flesh, you know, meat is murder, then I would believe that you couldn't sit here while I eat this food. You couldn't sit there watching, you know? Say I kill your Mama. And say, well, I know you think I'm not serious, but say I kill her and then start eating her with a baked potato. You're going to go 'God, Lorenzo, I mean she helped pay for your college, I mean god, why did you have to eat her?' You know, you'd start screaming. Road kill would make you smash your car into a thousand pieces. Be serious."

Lorenzo eats meats of all kinds. He eats roast pork and prime rib au jus and goose pate with truffles.

Somewhere I have indicated that it is once again summer. For people like me summers are like dreams—they are what happens to us when we are asleep. Lorenzo works full time. This is the eighties. Full time means all of the time no breaks no vacations no thought for anything but work no matter if you don't have time to think about the last time you had a day off because you are rich or getting there and by god your parents didn't raise you to loaf around thereby causing the next depression and of course you have a headache, what do you think this is a party, this is life and school you thought was so hard, well life is a lot tougher and you work full time. His summers are like his winters except that he is hot. He is particularly hot because he needs summer suits. When he assembled his full time job trousseau, he was seduced by the lovely soft and very heavy wools. Here is a suit you'll know you have on. For people like me work as a matter of survival ceases to be a necessity in the summer. We sleep through the summer to such an extent (compared to our frantic other-year pace) that even though we work perhaps three or four hours a day in the summer and some of us take on real work, e.g., clerking at a convenience store, doing technical writing, selling clothes in silly little stalls in dinosaur malls, we invariably have twenty or so conversations of this sort on or around September third, "So, did you have a nice summer?" "Oh. Yes, although I didn't accomplish a thing. I just sort of played around." "I read some novels" "Glad to be back" among the living, the waking. Despite ourselves we are ashamed of ourselves. We are ashamed that we never do anything.

Because this pattern of living and dying, waking and sleeping, has been my pattern for half of my life, I treasure my summers as that time during which I determine where I stand. Last year I allowed myself to say on the phone to someone, ah yes, I'm a narcissist, I can't remember to whom I said this, "Summers, when I accomplish nothing, is when I accomplish anything at all. I mean, you know, if it weren't for summers I would go mad. I have this theory, you know, that insomniacs and people who work full time are the same kind of person. They are afraid of the dream time and summer time they need to fill up so they don't go insane. Everything gets done in books, so if I didn't do nothing in summer I'd be too crazy to write . . . "Probably someone hung up on me. Probably someone said, "Yes, well, if you're quite done I have work to do." I don't care. I am convinced of this: summers make me who I am. Thus, I determined, as a matter of pleasure and not of survival, to artificially produce summer throughout the year. To this end I moved, with Lorenzo, an hour away from school. The city to which we moved has no major universities or colleges. We once lived in a city where we saw, on a daily basis, a man we believed to be

Thomas Pynchon, whom Lorenzo worships as the greatest living novelist and probably the greatest writer of ever and ever even though he is reclusive. How we loved to see him, or to see that person whom we believed to be him. We laughed with pleasure at his cars—whoever this person was, this person had a fleet of cars, all from the fifties.

I ramble pointlessly. That sentence refers to verbal wanderings but I also wander aimlessly on my feet. (On my feet! With my feet.) Because it is summer, in fact, I allow this rambling to go unchecked. There is a problem however and that is that with no aim there is no point and with no point no interest. The problem is that I do have an end. The point: there is a manner of thinking which interests me a great deal. The major thread in this thought is that besides the text, there is nothing. It is this nothing, say people who think this way, which must be explained. But, they continue, their tongue traipsing and lolling, high camp, the text is all that can be the case until we can begin an analysis of the nothing which will comprise everything but which cannot be analyzed in turn because in the face of our very being in the world it turns into text.

My point: one reason for this transformation of nothing into text is that some people, like me, lose their summers. They lose that time during with the text is far away in another world. They try desperately to make the nothingness of summer into something. My kind of summers are irrelevant. Everyone has a kind of a summer. Lorenzo, for instance, has a summer at the end of each week. These are the nothings he tries to assimilate with the somethings which make up a life. We can blame the dream work for the problem. The nothing of dreams—perhaps there are no dreams only the fictions we make into text in waking states—is explained in terms of mental or textual survival. I say no to the dream work. I say yes to dreams. (We can be the fish bumping into large white arms with scaly nose.) I try, despite my shame, despite my inability to understand the point, to create a story of summer out of nothing. The irony is that that story is now turned into the world of text—however, I do not run the risk of turning my nothing into something because, and this I promise, I do not intend to work. What follows is play, a summer's tale.

Nevertheless, and it must not be forgotten, one is torn. To play is a very serious thing in this sense: it is not only counterintuitive to play; it is difficult. Our socialization is towards work and specifically towards working within a text. Thus one is torn: although one wants desperately to play one does not know how.

4. "Everything, in so far as it is in itself, endeavors to persist in its own being" (Spinoza 1955, III,VI).

5. Important examples here are *ecriture feminine* and deconstruction.

6. Some of you may be unhappy that this will not proceed to be an epistemology. The death of certain self-consciousness is the death of certainty. Without certainty, epistemology seems to be *de trop*.

7. Giorgio Agamben in *The Coming Community* is a happy exception to the rule according to which I will be describing our profession.

8. I believe all communicative practices to share this feature.

9. There is nothing new in the process I am describing. What might be of special interest is the result of forcing ourselves to notice what we are doing when we write. The more we think about this, however, the more paralyzing it might become to write. If we are in fact writing ourselves writing becomes the most intimate thing. For some this is exciting; for others it is chilling. With the increasing use of electronic mail and bulletin boards as the area in which we express ourselves, print writing must also change. Copyrights are becoming increasingly complex and archaic. Names are also becoming increasingly complex and archaic. I predict an increasingly widespread use of pseudonyms. I predict that the privacy fetish in Foucault will get more and more attention.

10. "For example, when the British recently blew to smithereens the French fleet docked at Oran it was from *their* point of view "justified"; for "justified" merely means what serves the enhancement of power. At the same time, what this suggests is that *we* dare not and cannot ever justify that action; in a metaphysical sense, every power has *its own* right and can only come to be in the wrong through impotence. But it belongs to the metaphysical tactics of every power that it cannot regard any act of an opposing power from the *latter's* power perspective, but rather subjects the opposing activity to the standard of a universal human morality—which has value only as propaganda, however" (Heidegger 1982, pp. 144–145).

11. "Apartheid," says Derrida "The more it's talked about, the better. But who will do the talking? And how? These are the questions. Because talking about it is not enough. On such a grave subject, one must be serious and not say just anything" (Derrida 1986, p. 156). Here acting is talking carefully. "A serious response here would take hundreds of pages . . . " (Derrida 1986, p. 167). Here acting is writing enough. Derrida may be attacking people who rely on too crude a distinction between text and act, but his subsuming of action to text seems to rely on the efficacy of established channels of communication. This is why refining political strategies requires critiques of existing theories of political action, including, of course, political action that consists in writing. In this case, Derrida's strategy—there can only be the one—deconstructs itself in the world. For instance, in the de Man case, where writing is, after all, partly what is at issue, the same plea is made by Derrida as for understanding Apartheid. After an eloquent and moving defense of de Man's career and defense of text in itself Derrida engages in "action": "Having just reread my text, I imagine that for some it will seem I have tried, when all is said and done and despite all the protests or precautions, to protect, save, justify what does not deserve to be saved. I ask these readers, if they still have some concern for justice and rigor, to take the time to reread, as closely as possible" (Derrida 1988a, 651).

My criticism of Derrida here is that he does not go far enough into the world. Of course, it is better to reread, to rewrite, than to fail in these tasks; still, rereading, rewriting, should come to at the very least a new form of writing: emancipatory writing.

12. Socrates taking Plato in, e.g.

13. Bryan Short gives me this use of magic, which I find an interesting way to describe the sensation. Sometimes a better description would be "out-of-body." I do not believe in magic nor "out-of-body."

Chapter 1

1. Bill Nietmann and I have had fruitful discussions on Heidegger's probable thesis. I am grateful to him for these talks.

2. Well, I thought as I took the bus into Northampton. There

is nothing new under the sun. God or no God the argument against the meaningful possibility of following a rule just hasn't existed. Lorenzo was chattering about Turing machines and the reduction of all life to cellular automata when I got glimpse of a strange book: *Native American Anarchism*. God. I thought. I had no idea that AIM or like that were into anarchy. Thinking, cool, I purchased the book only a little surprised that Loompanics had published it. Always look into your books just a little before purchasing is a good idea. This was not about American Indians but about early anglo anarchy. Still it was interesting and I pondered this passage on the bus, thinking, well there is nothing new under the sun, and then weeping, a bit self-indulgently, thinking of Mary Dyer walking down the hall with Anne Hutchinson after the latter's excommunication. Both of them executed. Nothing new under the sun. The passage for your pleasure.

It was originally applied by Martin Luther to the doctrines which John Agricola upheld in a controversy with him over the interpretation of Law and Gospel during the period 1537–1560. Luther interpreted Law as a command accompanied by threats which forces obedience by fear. Christ and hence all Christians were not under the dominion of this law since Christ's supreme act of love had set men free from the Hebraic God's act of mercy. Christians, he maintained, lived virtuous lives not because of fear of punishment, but by love of noble precepts, precepts which were to be found in the Gospel. But John Agricola and his followers saw that the Gospel precepts were fast becoming law in the sense that Luther conceived it. They concluded, therefore, that the Elect predestined to salvation by God were free from and above the law, especially the moral code, God had written the laws on their heart; what they did, consequently, was good. The unregenerate were free from the moral code because they *could not* be good. Both the elect and the unregenerate were free from the law (pp. 17–18). Lorenzo will find this just so. He will say that God or no God this must be true.

3. It is worth noting that a contender for our century's prize philosopher, Theodor Adorno, is a mirror image to Heidegger in this respect. Adorno is not silent. He refuses, e.g., poetry for this century.

4. Irigaray filling up lack, Cixous a display of swirling-dervish-joyousness, Kristeva an increasingly private glimpse of the

self, Arendt a trembling power. Heidegger cannot *see* women in the clearing or elsewhere. I have heard experts argue that dogs are *dasein*.

5. "The End of Philosophy and the Task of Thinking" (Heidegger 1977, p. 389).

6. But Lulu has never really said *that*. It doesn't get to that point. Quilty has never said that. Humberto has never said that.

Chapter 2

1. Kathy Acker 1990, pp. 227–28.

2. Martin Heidegger 1977, p. 228.

3. Derrida 1978, pp. 251–277.

4. Allan Magill, *Prophets of Extremity* (Berkeley: University of California Press, 1985).

5. I am so ashamed. Well, there is no cure so certain for my shame than to confess all. I have been dishonest in the foregoing and (there is no end to how far I will allow myself to humiliate myself) I have almost stolen someone else's work. The pressures of she who is half student/half academic are overwhelming. Nevertheless, all things being equal—there's a phrase that says a lot—I do prefer not to lie and I do prefer not to steal. This is not to say that in all cases I am above these sometime mere peccadillos. To resume, all things being equal, the pressure to produce is immense—both internally and externally. Internally and externally!?

When Lorenzo and I moved to the apartment where we currently live—we moved here so that I would be forced to sit on a bus for a very long time everyday with nothing to do in order that I might retain my sanity—I found a manuscript entitled *The Paper Village*. This manuscript is what I was about to offer you as my Summer Tale. (Not that this would alleviate this god awful pressure. Nothing will because it begins anew every six months. All achievements erased; new beginnings. It's very religious. This pile of leaves would not even "count." It wouldn't even count because, well, its obvious. But it would count to me—even though it would have been stolen. Who would know that it was stolen? Nobody who cares. I could have said to myself, well, it doesn't count but this is because they don't understand. No matter how old one gets, how many degrees, it is always this THEY that chooses and decides. Not that this matters.) I was honest in principle although not in fact when I said that I would not work, I would merely play. I would play at bastardizing the text.

This is what I did not know when I wrote what you've already read, or that you started and then closed the book . . . no, if you are that you, you are nothing, gone, not a part of this text. How silly I get. How ashamed I am to be me. I had rewritten several pages of the manuscript I found before I wrote that other writing. Worshiper of text that I am, I had saved the original pages and copies of my changes in a file in the cabinet within which I keep political newsletters. However, two weeks ago in a cleaning frenzy, I inadvertently threw out those pages along with every newsletter dated before an arbitrarily chosen date. At this point I decided to repair the damage and try to find the author of *The Paper Village*. I cannot avoid mentioning the truth that I am not too, too sad that I am unable to return the manuscript. The woman who lived here before us refused to accept the work as her own—although it must have been. All the circumstances fit her. I've made numerous phone calls and the manuscript must be Anne's. She, Anne X. Stone, wrote it. And, now she will not claim responsibility for it. She was even rude to me.

I got her on the phone after I already knew that it was her work. It was during that conversation that she claimed to know nothing of the manuscript. Lamely she said, "Undoubtedly someone put it there after I moved and before you moved in. I don't even have a typewriter."

As if she couldn't have sold her typewriter! So I thought, well why not claim it. Why not? I cleared all conceivable obstacles to what some would call piracy like this: "Assume, for a moment, that you did, in fact, write the piece, but for reasons which are none of my business you feel inclined to deny any involvement with this text. In this case would you be opposed to my expropriating the manuscript for my own purposes?" She said that she was busy and didn't want to talk anymore. I couldn't call her back as she had made it plain that she didn't want to talk with me. The work is therefore now mine, to do with as I will and the lost pages don't matter. Still, however, it seemed only decent to add this explanation.

Decency, all things being equal, is an interesting topic. How easily I am able to say "all things being equal I prefer not to steal." How trivial a pronouncement. The theft of intangible property (I tell myself a manuscript is intangible like futures on the commodity market or computer thoughts) is tricky. One can steal ideas and phrases (memories!). But, all things being equal, very few would prefer to steal. How much better it is to have an idea of one's own. Even a paltry or skinny idea; even a great pondering lazy idea. But survival is interesting. In this bizarre world that I make my habitat (me, the god who makes worlds to live in, HA!) one must have ideas. It is that simple. To survive even on the silly level (here I am speaking of people like me who can occupy themselves with ideas because this silly level is not generally pressing in on them but who fear it as much as if it were because, fear being the glue of the media-state, one state under satellite, they are inserted into debt structures that mimic the silly level of survival this is not esoteric talk here—I am talking about GSL's, fractured fellowships, the back-breaking cost of books that one must buy for oneself because the library cannot afford to process their copies) one need not have original ideas. However, to survive psychologically, once one has accepted in part or in full a certain ethic, one must throw out an occasional witty idea in class, one must commit to text worthless ideas quite frequently and one hopes against all odds that one will have at least one significant thought in the course of one's career.

So, one convinces oneself that individuals are things capable of having ideas—not at all intuitively obvious when one dis-in-doctrinates oneself if only momentarily—and then one works psychological overtime convincing oneself that someone else's ideas are one's own. This is very hard to do because first, no one else has personal ideas in the first place, and, second, one is trained to remember where one hears specific ideas. One is tested in this ability. One is forced to write bibliographies and notes thanking people for their thoughts both those committed to text and those which one sees suspended in smoky air in a bar somewhere. This constitutes my excuse for the sin (sin!) of stealing Anne's work. One ceases to know what is one's own because the whole thing is a fantasy in any case.

And what a bad fantasy. Really one could do better.

You will forgive me, of course, for being so mercilessly boring about this and other issues. But it is worth noting that there is a controversy at present whether computer programs written jointly by professors (who according to one survey spent about eight hours making the lecture into a program) and computer specialists (who according to the same survey spend around five hundred 500! hours making the lecture into a program) are the intellectual property of the computer firm, the professor, or, the university that owns the professor. What is this? A reversion to the labor theory of value and property rights à la Locke or Smith? Labor time as a determiner of property rights! In a post-Marxian socio-economic era! Are we all mad? Couldn't we go mad in a more festive manner? I am perfectly serious. Couldn't we just let go? let beings be?

I know a very nice family. The mother and father are appropriately matched. She is kind, witty, assertive. He is kind, witty, assertive. They have four children, three of whom are "successful"—we know what this means—ranging from wildly so to moderately so. The moderately successful son is only thirty-two and will become wildly so within the next five years. The two daughters, being older, are already wildly so. They are a nice Bourgeois family. We know what this means. The youngest son, at twenty-six, is nice enough but he is not appropriate, does not understand the concept. He has no job. He takes unexpected and inexplicable trips which HAVE NO POINT. He doesn't have a plan.

This very nice family are photographed together whenever they assemble—once every two years or so. When they view the proofs, the mother is often struck by how very strange they all look. Their eyes askew, their expressions enigmatic and eerie as if they were looking at the blue fish on Venus. All, that is, but the youngest son, who, she muses, at a loss to explain this phenomenon, is incredibly photogenic. Gorgeous. Sane.

And aren't we all somehow at a loss here? Why am I free and others in prison? Why do some people get to say things like "all things being equal" and have others take them seriously for this talk? Why is one child always considered to be the 'other' child, and why do so many adults remember themselves as that child? Why are parents, of all people, allowed to make decisions concerning which children are committed to hospitals for observation? Why did I find the manuscript? Why was Anne there in the world with time to write something she didn't even care about? Why are there people who are kind who have no theories? Why is one person blindingly kind, another bitingly cruel? What did I do that allows me to spend my days and nights clicking away such questions and what did another do so that the essence of that person is to find material sustenance? Why does the media-state allow everyone to believe that rock-bottom this is what life is? Why do so many believe what in the face of evidence turns obscenely laughable?

Nietzsche, it is easy to turn to theory, especially anti-theory theory, says, "Any explanation is better than none." And yet, is a crucial point missed? Namely, that when one revalues or whatever one does which is to revalue (e.g., to steal to survive) one is torn. Will to power is an explanation. It is not a practice. It is one more explanation. Perhaps we will have arrived when we can say not "Perhaps people will rise even higher when they once cease to float out into God," nor, "I'm afraid we are not rid of God because we still have faith in grammar," but, "Nothing is better than any explanation," and, "I am afraid ... I am afraid that our language has created a falseness of perception, viz., that we exist."

And, the sad truth is that we do not. We have killed ourselves unknowingly. Computers teach at the university and worlds hang on trees. Will this addendum never end? The last sentence (not question) is surely a concluding one! Bear with me. What else will you do? Listen to static? Play with your TV set? I have a need to fully (at least more fully) explicate my shame. I am putting off intentionally the moment at which you turn to Ms. Stone's manuscript. She is more lighthearted. Mostly, she is more honest and it shows and I have falsified her document. I have dirtied it because I was jealous of how light it was and that it was an original (not a copy) and she left it and she had an idea. She is alive. She does something and moves on. I love her and want to see her. On the phone her voice.

This note. The pretentiousness of it. It sickens me. Throw it out Kelly! Write a preface. An honest short preface. I found this text. I contacted the author who has a voice that is a purring of a million volts. Here it is. A piece of text. I could go on, modestly, that I am public spirited, that I offer this text to the world. It exists, it is in language, it is readable.

There is no reason to continue this. I give you the text. The text that I have ruined. But perhaps it was already ruined. Someone could have lived in this apartment during the two months it was officially unoccupied. Perhaps the manager of the building took away pages she found offensive. Lorenzo may have played around with it. I am ashamed that I do not remember even where I have made the changes. I retyped the whole thing because I was going to pretend to Lorenzo (yes, to Lorenzo, the person with whom I live and to whom I referred, honestly, as my best friend) that it was my work. Such are my psychological insecurities—I'll share them, our's. They run deep; they run under cover.

Given the right circumstances I could convince you that something else happened, e.g., Lorenzo could have written the whole thing as a joke on me or I could have written it while blacked out, etc.

6. Deleuze and Guattari team up to describe Nietzsche. They write:

If some conspiracy, according to Nietzsche's wish, were to use science and art in a plot whose ends were no less suspect, industrial society would seem to foil this conspiracy in advance by the kind of *mise en scene* it offers for it, under pain of effectively suffering what this conspiracy reserves for this society: i.e., the breakup of the institutional structures that mask the society into a plurality of experimental spheres finally revealing the true face of modernity—an ultimate phase that Nietzsche saw as the end result of the evolution of societies. In this perspective, art and science would then emerge as sovereign formations that Nietzsche said constituted the object of his countersociology—art and science establishing themselves as dominant powers, on the ruins of institutions.

Why this appeal to art and science, in a world where scientist and technicians and even artists, and science and art themselves, work so closely with the established sovereignties—if only because of the structures of financing? Because art, as soon as it attains its own grandeur, its own genius, creates chains of decoding and deterritorialization that serve as the foundation for desiring machines and make them function (Deleuze and Guatari 1983, p. 36).

7. See Friedrich Nietzsche *On the Advantages and Disadvantages for Life*.

8. In my small town the leader of one of the thrash bands is ABD (all but dissertation) in Philosophy. She says before playing a cover of some death metal song: "Here is something we wrote on the way over."

9. It may seem very strange to you (yes, I mean you who are looking at this book in a library and are paging through it to

determine if it will help you pass one more night; and you who are staying at your parents' house because you are just too tired to drive home even though you promised yourself not to stay with them because it makes all of you nervous and now find yourself in your younger brother's room because he is on vacation and you are no longer tired because you miss your lover so much it aches so you reach for one of the books you didn't take with you when you left home in a fury seven years ago; or you who just read any damn thing; or you whose friend lent you the book to read on the plane) that I am writing to you. And, decidedly it is strange. I don't know you but I have the following problem: I don't know anyone in this city. The city where I live with my body. Of course I have my acquaintances at work; however, they are prohibited as friends because they are adolescent boys. I have no problem with making friends with the boys at my school but I am prohibited by the new conventions of morality. Translation: if I show any emotion other than disapproval or abstract encouragement to these young men, I get fired.

But it is strange. I do not know you. At least you may know me. (Already you have formed judgments. "Oh Christ, she writes as therapy. How passe. How, well, tasteless.") That is, I can try to reproduce a radical translation of myself for you, and if we end up speaking in a fairly close analogue of some relevant language you may have the conception of Anne Stone. That is my name. Anne Stone. I love it. My name. The god (to be introduced below because if you are to know me you must know the members of the paper village) says that I am very lucky not to be 'Ann.' 'Anne' is so much better. The god and I know 'Alison's whose parents spelled them 'Allycen,' 'Christopher's who are forced to sign themselves the feeble 'Kristoffer' . . . It is too awful what parents do to their children. My middle initial 'X.' stands for nothing. It has played an important role in my life—it has—because I met Xavier because his 'X' had letters following it and I asked him.

My background: I was raised to be a serious protestant. I am not. I no longer feel particularly angry. But I was in rage for years. It was so unnecessary. It is not as if this protestant thing went back for generations or anything. A whim of a grandparent for Christ's sake. My life. So I was raised with prohibitions, undefined guilt and let us not forget how much serious protestants (many, not all, of them, I'm not prejudiced, read their books, I'm not just making this up, I've lived this) hate women. I guess that's the worst. The X with nothing behind or after it. The hatred of women. The guilt because the hatred is cloaked in innocence: the gaze pretending to be love. So this is my background. A family, a community, a church. I teach, as indicated, at a very average, well maybe a little worse than average, boy's school. Imagine if you will my horror at having this be what I do. This is not the profession I would have chosen for myself.

Now you know me and you know what I do—although you do not know what I do because although I do not believe in intellectual elitism (I do not even believe in intellectuals—unlike many ex-protestants I am not a serious humanist or any of that long and painful re-protestant-ization of the ex-protestant) I do know that I find myself in an untenable situation. That is, I have no possible friends in this city and yet I am a social animal.

So you cannot know me because I cannot be myself. I live in a small city which is small enough and old enough that there is no place in it for me. I love, for instance, and among other things, to talk. I pay almost as much for the use of my phone as I do for my rent. I talk on the phone to old colleagues and high school friends. Additionally, I have a massive correspondence. It is not that I write so many correspondents; it is that the ones to whom I do write are all of the dying breed of serious letter writers. I have thousands of pages of letters that represent, along with five or six old plane tickets, and, of course, my phone bills, Ms. Stone's social life of the last two years.

I am very lonely. Xavier. As noted, I was initially attracted to him because his 'X' turned into a scrawl of letters which meant a name at the bottom of a page which page was handed to me by a friend. It was a poem. Oh in those days we sat in each others apartments alive with the possibility of the world and read revolutionary poetry to each other and planned marches and came home after demonstrations to talk tactics. And the poem was not very good but the name. Oh God. I said that I had to meet this person. It was also at that moment that I broke the barrier to bisexuality (I mean I knew that I wasn't just experimenting or any such thing) because I couldn't have cared less if X. . . were male or female. But then it occurred to me that it had never really mattered. Not at all *for me*, if you know what I mean. It only mattered in *other* ways. But then I never understood "sexuality." What could it *be*? In any case, in this case, it couldn't have mattered less. I wanted X . . . But Xavier went by the name Zack.

I was married to him for almost as long as we lived together prior to getting married. I still love him very much. He is one of my correspondents. We were divorced because of problems about children. I am and will remain childless. We were divorced, I divorced Xavier, because of a conflict about the meaning of childlessness. Xavier wanted us to have a child. I tried to explain to him, but failed to so explain, that for me not to have a child required an effort of will not unlike that I imposed, when, being severely depressed my senior year of college, had nonetheless to concentrate on my studies. Specifically, I had to write, in next to no time, an Honor's Thesis on the ethics of international diplomacy—the virtues of lying, I joked—and I was clinically depressed. I have wanted a child much more than Xavier ever did or could—I willed myself out of that desire.

The day I knew we would separate went like this: I was in a pose I had consciously adopted from my grandfather. Slightly slouched, legs crossed, once at the knees, once back around at the ankles, staring out the window with a cigarette in my mouth. I was thinking: "See, here is the thing: to concentrate enough to collect, sort and then spit out that which must be spat requires an effort of will not unlike the will of a woman who refuses to reproduce."

"You see," I said to Xavier, "I refuse to allow any of my creations to be destroyed by them."

Later I say to Xavier,

"Let us just say that there is repetition of some kind: How could one stand to live through the guilt of reproduction again?"

There is a new religiosity. Even the courts recognize it. Everything does repeat, if not cosmically then psychically. Although I am not sure of this I suspect it strongly. In a repetition, albeit not precise, of Pascal's wager, I live my life as if it were the case that everything will repeat. This is why I had to divorce Xavier. (It is why I had to quit my job—if everyone said to herself or himself: this shame I feel right now will repeat, it would be a better world. The worst ideology of all time: this too shall pass.) Xavier said that he rethought the child thing. He had changed his mind. But this sort of change is not the sort one can verify. In any case, I act my life out as if each moment repeats, is REAL, is not fleeting. Take childbirth. Take a moment of being Mama. There was a time when some humans—I don't believe that anyone believes it now—believed that the act of parentage was fraught with the guilt of that Pair in the Garden. Thus, each person born carried the guilt but the guilt lay most heavily with parents. Some persons passed through existence at the lower level of guilt by entering chaste relationships with God. These persons did not reproduce. That was the idea. The new guilt is godless—it is the guilt of bearing a hopeless child—a child doomed through no fault of its own. Thus, some persons will themselves guiltless of this particular kind of species guilt. This is the effort of will to which I referred when I said to Xavier:

"I will myself barren. No one can ever make of my child a person necessarily in despair. Look what happened to Sarah. From laughter and love to murder and despair."

Worst ideology: I am the only person to see through this. To concentrate hard enough to spit what must be spat requires an effort of will not unlike that which is required of a woman to refuse, in the name of principle she must accept a function she has no definitive reason to believe is not an intrinsic function of her self. She deforms, perhaps, her self on principle, perhaps. Why? So she can live a life worth repeating. Why? So that on balance there is more good and less bad in the world. I mean Xavier could have asked whether we might adopt a child. In which case it would have been yes my love yes my love yes.

I know the suffering of self-deformation. (Not just in the specific instance mentioned above.) The natural pose becomes that of the grandfather; slouching slightly, gazing at nothing, the body rasping. With an effort of will, the likes of which he had not undertaken, the likes of which he had never had time and energy simultaneously to undertake, he could have focused on a thought to describe his life: the granddaughter can so focus, ever the voyeur she is, and she finds the thought the gaze contained: work to survive, survive to die. The grandfather who loved me so much that the thought of that love changes my breathing pattern. And yet, when he was dying, from the dust of his labor, sticking in his lungs, gumming up his blood, choking out his life, I the granddaughter who wanted to love him back to give him the feeling of being thought more precious than any other thing, fainted. And then he died.

So I recognize that as I complain about my job at the mediocre boy's school, I am ridiculous. That my worries about reproduction are luxurious worries. I watched my grandfather die from his work before he could retire. The mine worked him, literally, to death. And I know that he worked to death at a relatively late age statistically: fifty-seven. Some are worked to death in other places at fifteen. Or some other ages. I recognize that my situation is relatively and remarkable easy. This sort of recognition and the speculation about cosmic and group injustice which accompanies it does not ease my personal pain. I've never understood why I am supposed to feel better because someone else is suffering more.

Back to the children. And Xavier. Xavier and I did not argue about the children really. Just the two conversations. His wish/my will. And then the reconsideration conversation. Later in the day of the wish/will chat, Xavier told me that he had changed his mind—the idea was just a passing fancy. A passing fancy—my life! a child! The next day I filed for divorce and that was that. I sold the house and that gave me two years of graduate school. And that was that.

You know me. Little by little. You know what I do. You know one of my correspondents. With such a correspondent, why am I writing you of whom I know nothing? (I know something. I know you who being listless and hungry left two pages ago for a dish of ice cream and now read this on the floor, ice cream dish in front of the book. And you, having not yet been described by my asides, who are convinced that I am merely guessing at the activities of the recipients of my letters. Don't be so smug. I am trained in the social sciences and , being lonely, go to movies, read newspapers, journals, demographic studies. Some of you are trying to remember where the silk cord is. Will she find it? Then what? Some of you have decided for the twentieth time that tomorrow you will leave him, her, them. I say DO IT. Don't wait for tomorrow, just pack an overnight bag and go. Nothing could be worse than a situation from which you have decided to leave more than twice. On the bus write the five things about your old situation you cannot tolerate. NEVER TOLERATE THESE THINGS AGAIN. I'm serious. Right now. Get out right now. Clear out the bank accounts. Seriously. What have you got to lose? Everything. Your kids. The approval of your parents. All right so I don't know anything. One step at a time. Take what and who you need and find a place for one night. One step at a time.

I do go on. I write to you because my paper village no longer satisfies—me or any of us. We want more. It has become too much. I am unused to so much emotion, having been in isolation for so long. Thus, I need to make my distance complete. Thus? Well, the logic is this. I am in the middle of something very emotional. I have forgotten how to be emotional. I need to purge myself of the specific emotion (i.e., that which explodes around the people I know) by letting out the general emotion (i.e., that to you) so that I can resolve the climax of emotion. That was wrong. That description does not work. What I need is a space for writing. I need this special space where I can write into a void. When still in graduate school, I satisfied this need through the material I wrote for publication. Writing into the void. I am afraid of what can occur to us (the friends—friends!) now. We have realized that it is very easy and relatively inexpensive to visit each other much more often than we have in the past (deregulation and all—so its unsafe, it's not like any of us are dying to stay alive). We will be in closer material contact. I am frightened. I feel so little like myself. Can I still talk? Can I sit in a restaurant with a group of people and chat? Certainly, I talk in class every weekday. But it is no more talking than is writing letters or conversing on the phone. I fear my face will have no expression, that I will seem as artificial as I have become. I must pretend an authenticity; it appears that I can't remember how this is done. I am practicing distance with distinct purpose: this is what I am doing here writing to you. (You are saying, well what you need is to practice talking. Well, damn it, one does need an interlocutor.)

We must change the tone. I will certainly become depressed if I continue in that vein, and, in any case, the fact is that the emotional climax referred to above, cannot be explained until you have some idea of the principals involved. Furthermore, now is not the time to go into it (i.e., the emotional climax) because I am feeling the woozy, unstable way I begin to feel when I contemplate the immaterial nature of my life. Non-fleshy. Yes I know, paper is as real as flesh and behind the text is the fleshy hand and the pulsing brain. (Ugh, what images. It is as obvious as if I wore my sex organs on my face, how little practice they are getting. Pulsing throbbing fleshy BRAIN???)

10. I will not give the name of this repressive organization.

11. So, strange, strange happenings. I was out walking and decided to stop at a record store into which I never go. A zine called K-Bone caught my eye and I purchased a copy along with some Crass tapes and some other stuff, a jogging bra with skulls on it, which I thought carried with it just the right hyperbole of irony. You know. Anyway, I get home and the zine is edited by only one

person, Anne K. Stone. What a bitch. I mean really. So I'm just sending her the whole thing. God I hate her. She is so perfect. So bye. I'm just going to send her everything. I don't want any part of this anymore. I am going to make her take on all the things that she is shirking. I didn't *ask* to be me. I didn't ask to have to write on her back, so to speak. Well, bye. Off her back. Lorenzo says I'm over-reacting. Xavier is probably perfect too!

12. I owe the idea for this "scene" to David Sherry.

13. It is strange to see my words again. I can't remember writing them like this. That awful woman Kelly Elliot has sent them back to me. She has spilled food on them. There are coffee rings on the pages. She has ruined my tone. It is not true that I don't care. I do. Listen to me through her:

At her worst she would talk to her hair. One could call these lapses symptoms of an artistic temperament or one could simply dismiss them as irrelevant. The interpretation one places on these, her worst moments, however, tells a great deal about one-self. If one excuses these musings as symptoms of a woman's malaise then one must believe in souls or in minds or in selves; that is, one must believe in some separate space wherein one is completely alone yet still alive. If one considers that Anne talking to her hair does not matter then one does not believe in anything. Only that which happens in shared space matters. If you believe that only shared space matters then you have never really experienced shared space. Shared space can be seen to be, when honestly encountered, a creation of an individual, spread across an encounter like a shield. If you have only encountered shared space in an unconscious way, that is, if you have never really experienced shared space, then your belief in the same is the result of a transcendental argument. I have nothing against transcendental arguments per se: my point is merely this. If your beliefs depend on transcendental arguments then there is a sense in which you do not believe in anything. If you think that me talking to my hair does not matter then you do not believe in anything. Let me describe myself talking to my hair. Perhaps you will see yourself in the description.

Everyone talks to objects. "Fuck you," we say to a chair. This is not strange. The chair is a social object. Every chair is a social object. (Notice how easily we can rack up universal truths if we become sufficiently trivial.) Likewise, or at least, similarly, everyone talks to her or himself. "Fuck you," we say as we stumble into an unseen chair. Or "What are you doing?" *sotto voce* as we spill unconsciously into a room having forgotten the point. However, if everyone talks to their fingernails, for example, we do not know about it. "I wish my nails would grow," is a possible and mundane instance of talking to oneself. But do we say, "hurry up and grow" seriously to our nails *qua* nails? At my worst, I say this sort of thing to my hair with complete candor: "Please dry. I need to go for cigarettes and we cannot go until you are dry." Notice that this is not an instance of me talking to myself. When someone finds the difference between hair and a chair, the latter which is necessarily and trivially a social object, we will have found the nothing. My friend Tim, now a celibate, knows that the body is related to the nothing. This explains why he does not like the way bodies smell. And feel.

The nothing is a blend of the human body *qua* body (not *qua* corpse . . . don't you just hate when they say "police have found the body of" and then some person's name. As if. And yes, I mean you, who are wondering if you've been had. Have you just checked the back of the book to make sure it says fiction and not something gross like sociology or philosophy. And you who read the most disgustingly violent, and violent in a sexist manner works of detective fiction but get all bleary eyed and sad when you read in the paper about some disgustingly violent *fact*. Hey, you tell me what's fiction and what's not. You, who say to the compilers of demographic fictions that you read to relieve tension. Hah! What do you do when you're nervous? I watch TV or read fiction. It makes me feel better. It makes *me* sick.) The nothing, to resume, is a blend of the human body *qua* body and the space which cannot be social. I have failed to describe myself talking to my hair. It is personal and I do not know you well. It is more than its being personal however. It is something about me that you must know if you are to have even a rough idea of Anne Stone but it is something that I have an indescribably hard time trying to intuit let alone re-describe in language. Two questions surround any attempt at such a description. One is "Who can tell me precisely why my mind is a social product, a chair is a social product, paper tigers are social products yet my hair *qua* hair is not? (Obviously in some sense my hair is social: I have it cut; I own a blow drier; its cells evolved as protection and as provocative ornament; I use shampoo. And conditioners. Mousses, gels. Dye to wear one night to a club and then to wash out that very night leaving a magenta streak on my pillow case.) Somehow my hair is as different from my mind as it is from my chairs. It is a property of me; it is inanimate; I talk to it when I am at my worst. The other question is "why do I *know* that these are my worst times?"

A question which remains, because we cannot find the difference, is: do we dare invade the nothing? Can we stifle our boredom? Can we find these moments about which no one daresto speak? (I am writing to you about them . . . this is the level of the fear. You who don't even follow the rules of etiquette as you read this believing yourself alone, you eat your snacks with a disgusting abandon in your solitude, or, you are like me and make of all your solitary moments the height of ritual: even a snack of an olive placed on a small plate with a crumbling of feta cheese, for color the smallest pepperocini in the bottle, a few water wafers, just so you won't be ashamed of inhaling the olive like a monster, like someone who has to eat olives all by herself in a strange town . . .) More importantly will these moments retain their nothingness if they are translated into text—the most social of objects? Why is the most social of objects the most artificial?

Don't lose interest! I'll make this more fun. You must read this. I need you to read it. I know that I am boring. Please don't lose interest. You are thinking, how dull she is. That nothing stuff, now there's something interesting, but she's a little out of date. You're right. I'm out of date, out of synch, forever waltzing to a tango. You are thinking: Lautreamont already found the nothing. And others. These are your thoughts. How you make me laugh with these puny thought of yours! Lautreamont! Hah! The feelings Lautreamont expresses are something with a capital and unattractive "s." They can be shared. They count as actual experience. Earlier in my life I had thought that the nothing was the shared embarrassment of two or more people when they find their objective and objectified hideousness. But this is precisely something. Experiences like these build character—they are shame inducing certainly at the time but no shame is felt in transferring them to text. They make up edifying discourses. See me mistreat Regina and learn! Notice how pale the paltry "See me talk to my hair and learn!" is by comparison. It is chic, even, to describe in great detail how one engages in sadistic sex withone's mother. See me sink into feigned depravity and learn! No, your thoughts make me laugh. But how boring a laugh it is, feigned and forced and feeble. And really, who hasn't been intimate with her mother? It's so boring. These men looking at post cards with their mothers.

The nothing is only that private moment of madness, of selflessness, so mundane, so commonplace, that it passes unnoticed. We have to make the moment up afterwards because it is so boring. Each such moment, nonetheless, borders on significance but we cannot grasp the meaning because it bores us too much to contemplate it even for an instant. It bores us to death. And yet I don't know you well enough to insult your thoughts. I apologize. Several years ago I too, like you, you with your puny thoughts and your erotic novels, thought that Lautreamont had found the nothing. How could I have been so wrong. The shark! The mother! The lover!

Here is a moment of nothing: some nut contemplates Abraham because he has nothing better to do. He freaks out. Much to do is made about how all this very heavy stuff is going down but it is too much to talk about. Why? Because nothing happened. This is a private freak out. It is an encounter with nothing exactly like the encounter with my hair. What can one say about contemplating Abraham alone and then freaking out tangentially? The significance is retrospective. A moment ago, I with my body alive did not exist. I was nothing. Well, you might say.

Well indeed. Let's talk about the special nothing of women shall we? I will say something about the plight of North American women. All of these women who are not agoraphobic are heroines. And so are those who are—but in a different sense. Another universal truth easily had. The agoraphobic women are those with sanity but sanity does not make saints, heroines, poets. Nothing is what each woman faces, briefly, right before she leaves the space she has foolishly but necessarily allowed herself to believe is safe from them. It is the flash of insight during which she knows that nothing is worth what she will face at their hands. (But it is not the nothing which implies everything that is the locus of the bravery. The bravery exists in the continuing to live.) The nothing is the fear of them when it is still unconscious. Later we reassemble this fear into something less frightening. We fear the fear of being humiliated, taunted, jeered at, stared at, grabbed at, raped, tied up in some basement, ignored, and so on. These are real fears. They do not stem from paranoia. They are not irrational. These are real fears we face. But there is a deeper fear and we experience it each time we leave our space—those of us lucky enough to have a space.

It cannot be shared this fear—even amongst ourselves. The shared fear we do share is the real fear. But the underlying fear of the fear of the fear. The fear that makes us hate men who write about women in two, not one, novels complimenting on each other's appearance by reference to their desire to be raped. Oh yes, you know who I mean. Those men who write about women's joking desire to be raped. The fear of the hatred of those men.

OK you might say. Enough of the women angle. You are tired of it. It makes you nervous. Do you know what makes me tired and nervous? Flashes of nothing? No. I've already told you that we create the nothing in retrospect. Nothing is simply nothing. To be tired of nothing is to be tired of one's dreams. No. I am tired of discipline. Let me tell you about my upbringing. (Oh god, you say, you already have. It is important. It bears repeating. I will tell you again.) I was raised to be a serious Protestant. Everything else about my upbringing is irrelevant to the discipline point. I am talking here that I was raised to be proudly humble, considerately meek, wealthy but poor in spirit. Rich if I had to marry for it. That's what it meant. Don't think otherwise. Not for a minute. The point of serious Protestantism, its repressed meaning, is to force women to marry men who have a little bit more money than they do. Why do you think that ex-Protestant women run away with violent motorcycle men? It's not guilt you idiot! Can't you begin to see the pattern? Can't you see it emerging? We'd rather get beat up than live out this protestant meaning for and ultimately against our parents. But I get ahead of myself.

So there is this religious thing that makes me nervous and tired whenever I think about discipline. Lucky for me I got all that out of my system early—by about age 21. I know I'm lucky. That's better than you who are thinking, well, my parents are Protestant and I married Robert because I love him. Please. Get a grip on yourself. RUN AWAY is what I always say. Get the hell away from all that love. Just remember throughout this that I hate discipline. I loathe it because it robbed me of time that I can't regain. I saw the academic world crumbling and since that world had replaced my Protestant world I would not give it up in time. I gave myself goals, commitments, love affairs with discipline. Nietzsche the arch-Protestant: discipline: this is where we find the bridge to the overman, or some such silly thing. I have the following to say about discipline: be grateful if your upbringing forced it on you. At least you can do something. Drink without anyone noticing perhaps. Or drive too fast. Or play the piano moderately well but with a savage hatred. Each note sounding the forbidden sunshine, the games left unfinished, the novel under your bed that had to wait until you had practiced the piano. Maybe it taught you to feel guilty each time you look at a book or read a magazine or play solitaire or just look out the window without a plan. Or maybe it taught you to be polite in therapy. "Could be, doctor." What a wide array of talents discipline offers the social community. Maybe you bench press double your weight.

Ah, stop your thoughts. I hate your thoughts, puny and pointless. You have no right to think, "Oh my, Anne is so bitter." But I'll calm down. I'm not bitter. I'm angry. I'll calm down.

There are stories and then there is fiction. Stories (nota bene: I am now defining technical terms) are god's eye sorts of things. They are objective facts about a person's life tied together by some perspective or narrative which is what constitutes their objectivity. (Need I remark here that I am a relativist and that "objective" is used in a relative manner? Are there any hardcore realists left? Is there a corner of the world where scientism is returning to fashion?) Fiction is the text that represents stories. It, the fiction, loses the nothing of stories so that a life might appear coherent, so that a life is not too boring to read. A life has to appear to be either pointless or have a point and for this it has to be sufficiently un-boring to notice. Your memory is a story. "The Phantom of the Paradise" (De Palma, early 70s) is fiction. Good fiction. I have just given examples. Introducing technical terms is something I have academic license to do. There is no difference between academic license and poetic license. The latter is just more boring.

What ever has she done? She has made me . . . unkind!

14. And, of course there is not. This is a *fantasy*. The madness of a moment.

15. The strong artificial intelligence (AI) position is that a perfect simulation of intelligent behavior is an intelligence. Hilary Putnam has discussed the possibility of "radical translations" (Putnam 1978, pp. 55–57) and what better material for a translation of a philosopher than the texts thereof. Further, any computable function can be performed by a Turing machine (Turing 1936, pp. 230–265).

Any radical translation's behavior can be simulated exactly by a specific Turing machine. There exists a universal Turing machine, namely a Turing machine that can simulate the output of any other Turing machine, given the Turing machine's description and input (Shannon 1956). The interaction of any two or more such Turing machines can likewise be simulated by a particular third machine. Many artificial life programs involve multiple, interacting Turing machines.

Fredkin believes that all material phenomena, including human subjectivity are "programs" running on a cellular automata of unknown (and unknowable) scale. Fredkin's position is outlined in Wright (1988). A universal Turing Machine can be simulated by a one-dimensional cellular automata (Smith 1971, p. 339). Any given cellular automata can be simulated by a Turing machine having as few as two states (Shannon 1956). Since a Turing machine can simulate any deterministic system, given the physical skill and space, our Nietzsche and Foucault and even Spinoza are possible.

16. Absolutely incredible. Having my work back has been good for the K-bone. You know, I do 'zines, which means I send out a bunch of writing to a bunch of people—mostly political stuff to political people. All right. No big deal. Well I get strange mail back but here's a doozy from someone who hates her work. I like it. I type it in here. For you. Of course it is from Kelly Elliot. God awful name, non? I'm in affirmation mode. Affirm Kelly Elliot. I'm going to print it.

Dear Anne,

Liked the fifth issue of K-BONE. Will you print this? It's on disk if you want it. So you don't have to retype it or anything. It is absolutely bizarre how what one wishes to do is not what one does. Thus, for instance all I ever even wanted to do was write. I don't mean by this that all I wanted was to yup it up with hash-, black label-, and loft-types who pre-existed any urban gentrification and who are out-living it. I do mean playing the artist trip to the hilt. The energy, the loudness, the friends who call at funny hours and drop by for a few weeks. The people who listen to you read the words you hammer out of paper and watch gestures in bursts of private excitement you recall afterward, people you've met just once and already you are begging them to let you put them in your book and they consent because they "fuck with words" too. It (frenzy-ing it up with people—anyone—not caring if one is called provincial or artsy fartsy) is what I do well—or what I *did* well until I spent too long in school getting all my language disturbed and my emotions in check. Now I can barely write a sentence that is comprehensible to any but the most dog-faced, the most precious, the least, how shall we say, *mobile*, none of whom ever did anything for me and don't want me around in any case. (How soon we forget! They did some things for me. Covered me with degrees and hickies all of which they regret but only because they regret everything. "We regret to inform you . . ." Taught me to make a big deal over things more sane folk consider *de minimus*. The white canvas, for example or the oral defense. Taught me to drink, not for fun, but for maintenance. "We believe that you are self-medicating." Later. They say. As if they were threatening me. The whole notion of "party" too complicated for one all academicized-out: "maybe you could get them to give you Valium or something? What do you think? Xanax?")

It's not like I'm the only party harmed in all of this. There were other days and *those* were the days, they think, their pea-brains all fogged with vegetable soup and their teenagers' porn videos (Seven Scenes of Dying While Doing It), when the priesthood was the *priest*hood and we didn't have all these ridiculous females around with their soft breasty-westies telling us that, well, yes, we exist outside of a certain role, a certain sickness and feigning shock they all were when I admitted that I had never even had menstrual cramps until the university clinic took me off the pill as punishment for the fact that I smoke. Well, yes, the medical ones said, we know that you don't want to be pregnant. It might ruin your career. (As if *that* were the reason! As if I would forego the joy of making my own baby, of loving a child, of being loved unconditionally at least for awhile for a *job*. As if ever anyone had thought to herself: "Well, yes. No children. Might interfere with up the career." As if anyone would dare make that kind of equation!) Nonetheless, it is *your* health we have in mind when we tell you that we cannot possibly, in good conscience, give you another script for Lo-ovril, knowing, as we do, that you smoke.

Call me paranoid. If I'm paranoid then you explain why I needed an education to get PMS. For years and years twelve or thirteen times a year I would bleed. Period. That is it. Maybe get a little neck tension. Never cared for tampons much but at age thirteen I had one of those typically adolescent counter-cultural thoughts: I don't need this. Haven't since—even those little itty bitty ones made by women lovingly for women. So I go through eleven, twelve years with no problems "down there" as they say except when I've been raped which happens a lot more than anybody knows. I have a friend who cannot remember how many times she has been raped. This is not fiction. It is not because she blocks this. It is because she grew up in a small town and was afraid of hurting her parents. So anyway, I'm OK down there until I find out that the anger I feel is because of that. And the tension. And the sorrow. The weepiness that descends on me pretty often like a pall. And the fear too they are saying now. The fear I had blamed on the other thing.

I thought I was sad because of things like Bhopal and my not being able to identify with Dworkin. Or because of the people hungry in Cheyenne and San Francisco and Queens and Sri Lanka and Holyoke. I thought I was angry because men in my program *have wives* as they dare to put it. They have read a few books, for Christ's sake, and this is nevertheless the manner in which they still refer to those for whom they pretend affection. Oh, everything, every minutiae of academe is too little a thing to worry about, too big a thing to forgive. So I come to graduate school and learn that my motivation for action, my budding gender consciousness is to me what my budding breasts were to me. Hormones. Of course, I'm paranoid. What would *you* think? (The dream is of the two doctors there saying well the pill has kept her in check this decade. She thinks she's normal. The withdrawal and ensuing first clash with reality may kill her so I'll do the implant when I put in the IUD. The nurse says: Let's not do the implant. I'd like to watch this one hit reality cold turkey. She's physically quite strong but doesn't care; she smokes so she's like given up her right to any kind of total treatment. Besides I need a control group for my work. So? Can I use her?)

I've told this dream to my mother who says: "Kelly. I will not have you talk that way about your father's profession." I say: But Mama Its Just A Dream. To which she says "Did you ever think that for many women this is great, its a Great Thing, something important to them, that they can finally discuss this, the pain they go through each month. The pain maybe you don't feel because maybe you drink too much just like your Grandfather. Although God knows I've explained to you fifty times if its twenty that there are all kinds of genetic complications you should consider every time you sashay to the bar thinking to yourself how glamorous you look with your cigarettes and booze and God knows what all else— I'm not an infant. I know you've never had cramps. Too doped up. Did you ever think the whole thing, seeing others talk about pains we've all had, did you ever consider this is liberating for some of us older women who don't talk about vaginas every time you turn around with your dearth of underwear all the time and the way you walk around the house without so much as a smile to cover that body that gives joy to you perhaps but has caused a lot of pain to those of us who allowed our bodies to fulfill the function for which they were created. No wonder you don't have a pain with your pale prissy body that never gets used for anything you could ever tell me about. I've always had bad periods. Every month I first feel the ovulation and then two weeks later the cramping bloating depressing bit. I'm glad that PMS exists. That way we all know it is something we share. It is a clear thing to us."

So I say to my Mom after counting to ten, who after all not only expected me but carried me and loved me and God knows what else for every minute of every day for years and years and now I'm depriving her this pain that I hadn't known was there: "Well, why didn't you ever tell me? I mean about the pain." "I didn't know what it was." There had to be this ... clearing, I think, I think, ironically.

So that night I think, Okay, maybe read a little book or something. Try to get that conversation with Mom out of your head. And then there I am feeling all fuzzy and *in anticipation* for something new. I'm thinking Mama is right in some respects. Who cares if maybe some man wanted me to think about PMS? We'll just throw it back at them like we always do. Strength from oppression. My friend, Jesse, always says that by this point it just couldn't matter what they did anymore because we knew enough to turn each attempt at killing us back against them. They dump committee work on us. OK. We make committee work count by making it some space in which to bond with each other and also by taking it as time. Thank you. Obviously that means I teach one less course? If they went to school north of D.C. and east of Philadelphia *they* can't say no either. And she, my Mom, did not have to go to graduate school to learn this. She said to me once you fancy yourself for women's rights and didn't even deign to learn to sew. How in the world will you ever meet any women? Well we run in different circles and she said well in those circles those women are doing OK. You've got to make up your mind if it is you, you are trying to liberate or your sisters. Not that I think any of us need liberating she adds with a glance to see if I'm listening.

Worse than all the women diseases they gave me, following me around the hallowed halls watching my ass, asking my opinion on things they knew I couldn't make an intelligent comment because they have chosen an unfamiliar topic—this so that they can leer with a knowing look like well didn't I always say, and not too quietly either, that well its okay if you don't know—I didn't expect you to know. I'd rather have *real* PMS than have them condescend to what they perceive, since they have engineered it in order to so perceive it, to be my stupidity.

Well, the first thing I did after they told me I couldn't have the pill anymore was to quit smoking. It has been a year now and I miss it. I told my friend Cally what may have been true but what was at least a serious joke: "I miss them; they were the best lovers I ever had." Lorenzo said that probably the reason I had smoked was that the pill gave me the urge. (He is at least as personally paranoid as I am and he shares all his friends' paranoias almost instantly. Mr. Empathy.) I said, well, to get the pill one must spend a great deal of time in the waiting rooms of doctors' offices reading all those ads urging one to smoke. So the pill did give me the urge. And college, all eleven years of it, I've been here *forever*, gave me cramps.

And made me so that I don't have (a) sufficiently strong emotions, (b) sufficiently strong desires, (c) commitments of any kind—I can tell you fifteen plausible and five or six good reasons why any given principle is not one to which it is worth committing oneself. The intellectual in the bunch: well what about the principle of sufficient reason. Let's not be *booooooring* now shall we? The moralist: one ought not kill small children without a reason. I can give you fifteen meta-ethical reasons for not "saying" (really for not even "thinking") that principle. Furthermore, the principle of sufficient reason assures that no one can. But what if you have reasons for not holding the principle of sufficient reason. Well, then, what *is* the point? It is pointless to have this discussion.

I have a secret power dream that I am a little teeny baby who can talk in paragraphs. It comes from the baby judges Isaiah spoke of and because of my attention to Isaiah. One of my first academic friends—she was in graduate school when I was a young undergraduate—used to say to me that she loved me for my baby breasts and because I was a baby judge.

Jesse never says silly things like that. She tells me about raising her children and visiting her son in jail.

Anyway, Anne, what do you think? Will you print this? Does it say *anything new*?

                                        Love,
                                        Kelly Elliot.

17. Bill Martin wishes to replace cynicism with caring. Me too.

18. Imagine someone who is not so young. That person is watching. That person is counting cars from an apartment window. That person is feeling shame, guilt, not too much. Fifty six . . . I could be working . . . fifty seven . . . I could be playing . . . fifty eight . . . I could be overthrowing the state. Imagine someone writing this. Imagine the hands. The hands which resemble your own to such an extent that hands take on an erotic significance far beyond what one would expect: there is no secret to them being always exposed like so many faces. Almost like the sole of a foot they require a light touch. They are so hopelessly useful, so always at hand. Imagine the hands of lemurs picking at fruit frantically. Imagine all these hands so like your own that they are interchangeable. Open your hand.

> All solitary dreamers know that they hear differently when they close their eyes. And when we want to think hard, to listen to the inner voice, or compose the tightly constructed key sentence that will express the very core of our thinking, is there one of us who hasn't his thumb and forefinger pressed firmly against his lids? The ear knows then that the eyes are closed, it knows that it is responsible for the being who is thinking and writing. Relaxation will come when the eyes are reopened" (Bachelard, 1969, p. 181)

This matters. Our legs are not so alike, our brains. Think of the diversity of eyes, all bulging in their silence. A radical philosophy will necessarily involve the sense of touch at the most basic level. At root it is our conservatism, our fear, that keeps us from speaking.

Imagine writing or telling a story.

Chapter 3

1. Many of my friends and colleagues disagree with me about Acker's importance. The less computer dependent they are, the less they like Acker. Sexual practice and critical perspective have

little to do with whether one values the work of Acker or not. Obviously this note is anecdotal.

2. Well, of course, this "one" is oppressive. Portions of this chapter were read at a conference where several persons approached me afterwards to say that Acker alienates them, makes them feel sad—anything but rejuvenated, hopeful, etc. More on this reaction follows.

3. "Wherefore it is certain that those, who cry out loudest against the misuse of honor and the vanity of the world, are those who most greedily covet it. This is not peculiar to the ambitious, but is common to all who are ill-used by fortune, and who are infirm in spirit" (Spinoza 1955, V, Prop. X, note).

4. I use a distinction between social and political that is *not* the traditional distinction between private and public. Instead, political refers to state-formed or encouraged groups; social refers to community-formed or encouraged groups. There is, of course, some overlap in the categories. I view our most serious fight for survival as that between the social and the political. For survival to persist, the social must win.

5. For reasons that should become apparent throughout the text, anarchy seems the only plausible political configuration in late capitalism.

6. This applies, of course, to academe. We are, many of us, state workers.

7. And no, of course, I won't name names.

8. See the entire "The Will to Power as Disappearance," in Bey (1985).

9. People have laughed at me because I believe that laughter is a political category. Obviously I am not alone in the belief—I did not create the category. Their laughter is political. Writing without restraint changes the world. (A change in logic changes the world too, you know.)

10. I am not minimizing here what is often called material oppression. I believe that oppression of sexuality is material oppression and its actuality makes all other kinds of material oppression easier to perform.

11. See "Plato's Hystera," in Irigaray (1985).

Chapter 4

1. Julia Kristeva 1992, p. 285. What if we didn't know who "they" stands for here?

2. I wonder if I should print Kelly's latest in K-BONE? I sort of like it as a letter but I got the idea from her little introduction that she liked it as a feature of some sort. Maybe she is on to something about power. There is one thing I know about power and I figured it out for myself. Within limits, power is there for the taking. I don't mean that there is only so much power. I mean some people can't take it because they are starving to death or something like that (not necessarily that, its an example, hungry people, historically, have done more than their share of saying, all right, that's it, we've taken more than our share of pain). You want me to know something. You can let me know. Write about this and send it around in the mail. Somebody will put it on a computer billboard. I mean, get serious. All the print and most of it is written not by US but by THEM. But now we can change that. Power is available to be understood and then lived. There is more power than we use. With writing now, you can reach like a million people easily. You can easily BLOCK a million people's networks. WOW.I'm having trouble focusing lately. I can't believe that *you* are focusing and yet I need you to focus so I can make you focus. Your attention wavers from sharks to hand cuffs, from ice cream to feta cheese. As I get to know you, I think, well, how much of this should I keep personal, i.e., non-social. But this division into personal and social is especially artificial with respect to me. I do not mean to be vain. I do not mean to set myself apart from other people. I can only make sense (or try to make sense) out of what I see and out of what I observe. It seems to be that the division other people have between their private and public selves is more clearly demarcated than mine. It must be for there to be the sorts of jokes that there are about this distinction. (If there are so many such jokes, someone must find them funny, is my argument. As I spell that out I think: what a particularly bad argument!) Many jokes, though, are centered on this situation: someone, someone whom you love or who is a stranger, catches you doing something you normally only do in private. (Wolf down an olive choking on the pit in your haste.) (And then the closeness of public to pubic. Really.) The work of these jokes is that our private self is gross, disgusting,

unrefined, full of bad smells and ugly movement. Since this is the work of these jokes many people must find it strange to have the public (even the public of the significant other) intrude on their private doings. BUT I HAVE NO PRIVATE DOINGS.

Ever since I was quite young, I have been believed that I was being watched. Not by God. My grandmother died and a relative said to me something like, "Annie, sit like a little lady. Your grandmother is watching you. Wouldn't she be disappointed . . ." I was very young. I believed this relative. Few people ever explain to children why they say the things they do. I was around age five. I did not believe in God. If the relative had said, "Grandma is in heaven watching you . . ." there would have been no damage to my psyche. I could have tied this new lie onto the framework of what my brother and I called the BIG BLUE LIE.

And notice, please, it is not as if I were looking for my grandmother in closets or anything. I knew she wasn't really watching me. I believed in her death. But I didn't *know* that she wasn't watching me. How could I, at five, know something of that sophistication or magnitude. That death is the absolute. That she was absolutely gone. So, my private life is in some sense not private at all. As I grew older I realized that many things were simply more enjoyable if one assumed, or believed, if this latter intentional state were at all, at that moment, psychologically possible, that one was being watched. (Oh you of little imagination! Do I have to recount those things which are made more pleasurable by this fiction? Sex is the obvious one. A performance. Eating, alone, is much more enjoyable if one assumes that one has an audience. Each dish an expression of style, each flourish of the napkin gauged for the camera angle. (I'm not gonna wait around for you to play back, baby play back your love for me.) Exercising. Dancing to a record. Speaking on the phone. (The camera angles in, no running sound track, tears down the face, flared nostrils, over track with SSQ or like that.) Walking down the street as if the swirl of city and life were part of an impossibly perfect movie set. How well one turns ones foot in such a situation! How beautifully one grooms, or how magnificently one fails to groom, oneself. Swimming alone in a lake. Playing tenderly, ever so more tenderly now that the camera is softly focused, with a young child. Looking in a mirror.

But the above sense is not even the major reason why my private and social lives are blurred. I can make of anything another principal in the action. I talk to my hair—only at my worst—but this is not the extent of my creative capacity. Far from it. I have enough selves that I am my own city if need be. The great moralist informs us cribbing from some Romans that if we cannot do the just thing we must, at all costs, avoid society. (But then this same person is he who says that marriage is the promise to exclusive right to one another's sex organs.) If we cannot function without society we must create our own. My society is such that even when completely alone I can be unjust. I can be unjust to one of the many selves I create for myself in order to have something to call a public. No! This is not a simple case of imaginary play friend. I know, from experience, that it is possible to refract oneself so cleverly that one can, for instance, play gin rummy with oneself and not remember what the two, or three, people whom you have created for the game, have in their hands from one move to the next. You say this is mere child's play. It is perhaps child's play. It is not MERE.

So the public/private distinction is not so interesting to me, although I can see why the jokes about it are supposed to be funny. I would think that if one carried in one's head the distinction quite explicitly then the jokes would be more sad than funny. But here I superimpose my prejudices on others. Perhaps these jokes are deeply funny.

Some things are truly joyous. Joyous, you think. A facile word. A word completely thinned out from overuse. There is nothing left which can be properly called joyous. The reconciliation with god was called an anticipatory joyousness. Nothing can conceivably compete with what this must surely have been had it been possible. In spite of myself, on occasion I find myself wishing for reconciliation with something perfect. It is perhaps the most glorious idea ever thought. The best fantasy by far. Some think that because no such reconciliation can take place, nothing can be joyous. Doesn't academic life make fools of us all? What an argument. What total crap. But still, the absence of any consideration is foolish too. There are those who refer to such things as Fourth of July celebrations that they were "truly joyous." We have ruined the language. No more use from that word.

Well, in thinking those thoughts, you are perhaps correct. Before I considered your objections I had thought that it was joyous to see, after several months, or even days, a person whom one loves deeply. I had thought that it was joyous to exercise for several hours until ones body is elastic and shaking from exertion, and, then, to slip quietly into a warm and oily bath. I thought that it could even be called joyous to encounter an unexpected object of beauty. But you are probably right: I project, I pretend, I over-invest the past with meaning. (Nonetheless I believe that I often feel joyous. Perhaps I am wrong.)

Even though following from your argument, deep sorrow becomes impossible—after all, we cannot be deeply sorrowful at having been barred from the presence of god, whose presence we have never believed in. I know that I have experienced deep sorrow. Oh why did I have to be raised to be a serious Protestant. This means, to me, who else is there, that the ancestors of my parents believed in God and they believed in the Devil. They were afraid of both of these creatures. Furthermore, they knew what would happen to them if . . . Then came a generation of doubt which was still solidly in the tradition. Then came back those who did not authenticate their doubt and they come back with a feverish vengeance. These, my parents, teach their children that they are gods. They can't help it. Everyone else is limp and doesn't really believe this stuff so the fear turns into awe of self and awe of one's children. (Coupled of course with self- and child-loathing.) The children of these persons never for one minute suspect that there might be a God. They know there is no god. But, like their parents, they know what the Bible says. They read Hegel. They know what this Prussian state is, for Christ's sake. And they know that if there is a god or if there are gods, then they are those gods.

You are thinking, oh come on, no child thinks she is god just like that. Where did it come from? Didn't you read what I said? Was it too boring?

3. Deleuze and Guatari 1994, p. 28. Even more: "Communication always comes too early or too late, and when it comes to creating, conversation is always superfluous" (p. 28).

4. Hello again. I left you, I think, in the realm of the gods. A pantheist system is so much nicer don't you think? Everyone gets a chance to rule: it is a much more fair system. No one is left out. Everyone has an adequate place in the universe. I, too, have god, when I, myself, am not too busy being god to some worshiper of my own. There is even this one person, this god that I call god. Oh God. Understand, the reason this person is god to me has nothing to do with an ability to understand or recreate the world. This person is

god to me because a solipsism so complete exists therein. But. God writes me letters. Mountains of letters. God is insanely solipsistic. I'm no longer satisfied. I want this one in the flesh.

I check, as I write, for the mail. I can see the carrier's truck from my fourth floor window and then I and the other shut-ins, agoraphobes (we leave only for work and some of us . . .) look for our mail. No, right after I see the truck drive on, the doors creak open, I dart through halls and staircases, scoping my neighbors through peep holes, mumbling about bills, everyone enviously checking out my bundles and bundles of letters. Here is the stuff on power from Kelly *again*. I liked it, I was going to print it, I should have written her. Why can't I focus?

Dear Anne Stone,

You could have answered the last note. Oh, no, you couldn't have since it has not been long enough. Something else for K BONE? Do I bore you? I call this SMALL OBJECTS.

It is not as if the fear could be dissipated by staring and understanding small objects. Nor could one forget oneself in anything but breathless insanity. And, really why would one try to overcome the fear which, after all, reminds one that one is almost someone who is alive? Would it be that one wanted to enable oneself to continue in a larger more public madness if only momentarily? And even these questions were not seriously considered. The questions were not taken to be states of mind worth contemplating, worth overcoming. They were seen as snatches of language milling about, carrying the same importance as similarly formed questions about what to wear.

It is not even as if I cared. And, really, the irritating thing about my life is that even though I feel a deep lack of care about these and other issues I am constantly racked by the most painful anxiety and fear. I am almost constantly in pain and I remain not quite bored but still not quite engaged. I can see back to stages in my life as if they were punch lines in feeble jokes but I cannot imagine being myself now or then. I am certain of one psychological fact. When I can equate myself with the person living out the life it thinks is mine, I will kill myself into something else. When I can care that this is me and me is this thing then I will be able to do something about it. It is really pathetic. There is no possibility of engaging anyone in this story of borderline self-hood, near commitments, possible encounters. The only things about me which might contain some interest are the reconstructions of small scenes after the fact. These reconstructions no one believes partly because they are not true. Even so, even though they know my lips' mouth lies, everyone I know goads me into telling. "Tell the one about the guy in Montreal." If I had done the things I imagine myself as being capable of doing, I might have a life worth preserving as itself—a life that does not whine. If I can find a person to be or a person to know who NEVER whines, ah, there we have heaven. As anyone who has thought about it knows (read as everyone knows) the unrealized life is not worth living (but not worth dying over either). The realized life would not whine and would want to change itself into something else. Immediately.

It is irritating in this world to hear the whining of people who have the privilege to whine. Irritating. It is infuriating. Listening to the whining of the few who have the time for it looses rages long since forgotten. And yet it is a world in which it is impossible to both be and fail to whine. It is an untenable world and there are no other ways to look at it. We ought not mourn; we ought to organize. I agree! I embrace this notion. I second it. But it cannot be overlooked that there is an end to the possibilities we have for climbing out of this shit. It is hard to tear over when strains of glory are heard since we all know that it is really and truly hopeless. Look, I'll tell you the sort of despair we have. We have despair that is not even poetic. It denies all overcoming. By definition. Ours is a despair that bores deeply. We must struggle just to be civil.

It was a very liberating thing to have this pass. Lorenzo found it for me on the bus and it had about seven weeks left. It is a semester pass and it lets me ride all over Hartford on any of the PVTA buses. I think Lorenzo wanted me to say that he should keep it because he found it but it is made out for a high school senior female and I think I can play that role better than he can. Really, I can play any role better than he can. I do better drag than him. I just do. I make a better man, I make a better boy and I do better females than him naturally. It is hardest for me to be a girl. I hated being one and except for the first time (and only time) Cally finally said she loved me, my happiest moment was when I knew that I wasn't a man.

I told Lorenzo this once and he laughed and said I was deceiving myself because if I was thrilled to be a woman why the hell did I always bind my breasts and etc. He is such an ass. I told him that part of the "thrill" (what a way he does not have with words) of having breasts was to bind them on occasion. Couldn't he see that at least and he said no he didn't get it which goes to show something.

For a while I thought it was possible to overcome by focusing on the small. In memorizing the details of small objects and analyzing in depth the pettiest of relationships and mores I had thought to find the beauty de minimus that has sustained so many persons before me. But I have found one (philosophical?) truth: there is no longer anything small. (Oh pedant? Is that you reminiscing Pascal's infinitely large and small conundrum? Rehearsing the phrases to inform THEM that this (philosophical?) truth is not new?) The translation of this is of course that relaxation is henceforward impossible. Nothing stands alone.

Remember the fear that "the cheese stands alone, the cheese stands alone, high ho the derry-o, the cheese stands alone" engendered in us as children? And which among us relaxes? Did that count, that time several years ago when I fell asleep on the first try? Don't smugly think how defeatist I am the writer of this text that is too defeatist to be depressing. Certainly not pathetic in any of the senses. Defeatism may be a correct mode for this the cruelest of centuries. Consider this (philosophical?) possibility: everyone is defeatist. If everyone were defeatist then . . . Couldn't there possibly be an outcome of that eventuality less frightening than that from these "If everyone were insane?" or "If everyone were too afraid to admit defeat?"

Lorenzo gave me the pass and I'm happy to say that I lose more agoraphobia—the fear of the marketplace, I don't dare go to places where there are lots of people without making elaborate plans and disguises—every day. Yesterday I took the bus over to the Wadsworth Athaneum in my regular clothes and didn't freak out at all. It is scary living in Hartford because it is so rich/poor and there are too many people for the water and most of the people who live around here think it's a sin to be poor. I'd leave but I can't afford to get out of here. I think I'll probably die here and probably pretty soon because the land can't hold up all the filth for very much longer. The Earth has its own ideas about how many people it can handle and how much abuse it will allow and I'd guess it has about had its limit. I've had mine but I can't just close up on everyone; I have to keep looking for something to occupy me. My work doesn't take very much time.

A result of the translation (that there is no more small—pay

attention! this is not done for my benefit!) is that no one is sane.
Glibber persons than I could ever be think this is a cause for
cynical celebration. It is not. The end will only be that we shall eat
each other alive. There is no alternative for a species so glutted by
fear and so hopelessly interconnected each to each with hatred and
distrust. So in the meantime I try to stay alive as you all try to stay
alive. We watch our friends, enemies, families, neighbors and
strangers die hideous deaths and think well, I'd kill myself to avoid
this but I can't find myself to kill.

Here is what I do and it is probably why my natural paranoia
has turned into such an elaborate one. (My theory is that all people
have some paranoia and then some people develop a justified and
elaborate paranoia to protect themselves from those they have
harmed and some just naturally get sicker. By the time someone
is thirty or so they are in the one camp—the camp of the guilty, or
in the other—the camp of the mentally ill. If you're not guilty in
this world, you've gone crazy with fear that you might or that you
are despite your good intentions. Guilty people have lots of friends
that they hope don't meet each other (me); sick people stay home
a lot, leaving only to go to work and to buy food and stuff or to go
to their last trip to the hospital (me). Shall we talk about the
special cases?) What I do is act. I disguise myself, usually with
Lorenzo, and con people into helping me. Some people think I'm,
like, degenerate. Well, you know, fuck them in a way. I mean, I'm
not degenerate. I just like to meet and play out lots of people. So
where's the guilt? I guess my special guilt is in the disguises
because I wear the disguises in case I don't want to see these
people again. It is a safety measure but it is dishonest. I mean I
know that. So sometimes I meet people who need me and then I
like never wear the same disguise again because I don't need
people who need me. Except for Lorenzo. And Lorenzo is a friend.

No more of this you are thinking. This whining is really in-
tolerable. Who are you to whine? Go ahead kill yourself. Who will
care? And you have thought the same thing as friend after friend
threatens to kill herself, to hang himself, to join this or that army
and kill others. It is a death culture so permeated by the pulse of
heart beats gone haywire that we yawn when yet one more among
us threatens some violent act. It's you? I thought you were going
to kill yourself last week. What happened? Things are not so bleak.
I can't pin myself down so I remain alive. Things could be worse.

I meet pretty interesting people for the most part and we have lots of discussions. We talk about art a lot and most the people I meet are drop-outs from jobs or theaters or ballets and have taken what they think is true and beautiful to the street. We never say the word "art;" we talk about "sex" and about "passion." Drop-outs from universities talk about "desire" because for theological reasons of which they are mostly unaware, they cannot say "passion." People say after talking to me: "You don't have any passion. You only care about technique." This turns me on beyond anything normal. I love people to say this or its equivalents, for example, "you are detached—like a machine," or, "I get the feeling that your eyes are made of glass." My hair bristles and I get totally turned on by comments like these. Don't ask me why. Lorenzo will say things like "when you get to know her she is really passionate," which is total bull shit and he says it like he is making a joke. He makes people nervous when he talks this way and their anxiety turns me on. The most exciting thing I can think of right now is to be on the verge of grand passion—to change myself into something else, to melt into the color of someone else's scheme, to have thought a PERFECT PHRASE—and there, on the verge of greatness, on the edge of insanity to look at my eyes in a mirror. What I want to see in that mirror, what would push me into ecstasy, is the appearance of being about to die from boredom.

Do you like it? Will you run it?

Love, Kelly Elliot

Well, flesh. Have to write Kelly. Have to forget that last June god was breathless before me. I found this very exhilarating. I had arrived in a city (one sufficiently large that one could be assured anonymity) several hours previous to this encounter. God had said, "I think we should see for ourselves what this means, this feeling of fate we share." And I had said, "I'll come out. When can you see me? I mean, airplanes exist. They facilitate human connections."

So I was in this city where god lives and no one else knew I was there. I had just come to see god. And there, in the stifling June heat was the god breathless before me and I said, tritely, trivially, "I am glad to see you." The perfect thing to have done was to trick god. This is what I had decided to do. Sitting in a bar no one I knew in god's city would dare to frequent thinking: "How perfect not to show. In this the age of the they I would be completely lost to everyone who knew me or knew of me. I could disappear."

But instead here I am with god before me and god is breathless. The game with god had collapsed. I had let the solipsism play itself out. By anticipating the thoughts in the room. We are both well-trained social scientists; it is nothing to anticipate thoughts— I anticipate your's. I act in accordance with the wishes in the room. It is mechanical. We are automata. It's a game—the game of seeing how far the fantasy will take me. I am in complete control of this game. I have always made it necessary for this letter writer, this writer of missives, to believe fantasies are. This is hard to explain but it is like second guessing what someone wants in those desires that are not even articulatable to the person proper and acting out those desires for that person immediately. Thus, god was forced to believe what was only hoped or feared: that there was only this solitude in the universe. The evidence for this was there: I was perfectly what was desired at that truest level that is beyond words, I was the only true desired thing. Now I am going to reject the fantasy. I cannot be more cruel than this and I need to be cruel at this point in my life. It is necessary to me. I want this so unbearably. The flight has been a tension I could repeat and never grow tired over. I am the live wire.

And then I find that I'm not anticipating thoughts or any such thing. I am breathless before god. I am not play acting; I am not acting out desire. I've been alone for so long I can no longer act out—the feigned public emotions of the past have gone from my wardrobe, I have no public emotion left. So, I am breathless before god and I am not feigning. Mass hysteria for just the two of us and the blood beat is drowning me. This is the first emotion I have honestly encountered in the presence of another human being for as long as I can remember. The network of this game dissolves around me and I feel completely open and vulnerable. The maze of discipline has lost its power and I have no self, no play, no strategy, no ideas but one: I am breathless; the blood beat drowns me.

I came to god with nothing for nothing consumed by nothing. Five minutes earlier I was thinking, well, why not disappear? Why not? The thought which flooded me was,

"Maybe I still have a body; maybe I can live in the same city with someone I know."

You see how hard it is for me to talk about this. I desired cruelty and discipline. This was mind fucking at its apex and we could not sustain it. Breathless/blood/beat/body. One blood, one body. Why do we always forget the body?

I stayed for three days. We didn't speak much. The room we

didn't leave was heavy and stale. We drank a hundred scotches. We smoked a thousand cigarettes. We couldn't find out whose breast is this? Whose leg? And then I left. The taxi driver who took me back to the airport just said, "Hmm."

Well, I had better go answer my mail. Somehow I feel proud of myself in odd moments but mostly I feel as if I don't really have a . . . life.

5. I took yesterday off from you to catch up on my correspondence. I called in sick. I cannot get Kelly Elliot out of my mind. I mean at first I thought well she's insane, clearly, and in a not very interesting way, not to be mean or anything, but we have to choose whose insanity to take care of in this the age of free falling mental debris. I don't mean this in any nasty way. We could spend all our time taking care is what I mean and I thought well, Kelly needs help but who am I and like that. (Oh you, you help everyone you meet who needs help. Bully for you is what I always say. How does it feel to be PERFECT?) So I'm worried about this Elliot woman because, well, I just hope she's OK. And I can't write back to her because she never says where or who she is really. How could I have thought anyone exists qua Kelly Elliot. Would I believe there to be a person behind, say, Larry Derry? (Did I say that? That there is always a way to communicate? Computer billboards? Power is there for everyone. God, with friends like you all . . . I mean don't I just love those who remind me of the dumber things I say?)

God wants to see me again. I haven't received any communication about this but nonetheless I am sure of it. But I don't dare. I can hardly dare anything. There is a man who works in the small drug store where I purchase newspapers and items like that. He tries to be friendly with me but I watch the natural way he interacts with other clients (other clients! my neighbors!) and it is so different from the stiff manner in which he treats me. When he smiles at others he looks so nice I want to run and get in the line of that smile. When he smiles at me it is a smile of pity and it looks about to crack his face. I think, "Oh, well, I must look a proper monster. Perhaps I move in big lumbering insane looking steps, spinning on each fifth step in a paranoid sweep of the room, making sure no one is trying to stab me in the back, smiling in the shadows of signs that say 'we prosecute shoplifters' as if to inform the shopkeeper that I know he's just trying to bug me personally, then, laughing at the joviality in the store, as if to ask forgiveness for thinking that they might accuse me of shoplifting, sounding not like a friendly tinkly little bell but instead startling even myself with the low moan that comes out of me as if I were a beached whale."

So this man pities me and I see him on occasion when I buy my papers and I think, "Well, why not develop a taste for all those things I have been too *shy* to care for: National Enquirer, twinkies, generic cola in huge two-liter plastic bottles, beer that comes in the same set-up, day-old bakery goods, tabloids from England that give tips on how to give one's own self liposuction? He thinks I'm deranged anyway and who is he to glance at me, what has a PhD, as if I have sauce from dinner on my forehead? I don't, I don't."

I mean I never have sauce anywhere, I'm very clean and I never act inappropriately in the store so why the large space afforded me when I walk into it, why the wide-eyed glances, why the certainty deep within me that they, the they there in the neighborhood corner store, believe me to be the character of the neighborhood? And how does this relate to my hair? Or to god?

6. So I have issues to resolve. Real life issues and theoretical issues because I have hopelessly destroyed a career, and, consequently my social life. My mother would say I am childless, and, consequently my social life is such that I make of my real issues theoretical ones. And we are both right. My life is such that the stuff of it works itself out in print. (Well this is the age of a plastic confessor after all.) So I should pick up the phone and start making appointments but I feel as I if I can resolve this issue if only I could resolve the ogling issue.

You see, I can no more divorce my life and its problems from my femaleness than its existence (my life's existence, I meant, but also I guess the existence of the female in me, the female that *is* me? part of me?). The ogling issue worries me. Recent events and controversies have confused the issue. Ogling is what strangers do to women. I know, I know, men ogle men too and women ogle men. Women ogle women. I ogle women. I ogle god! I know this but think of this in gender terms. I am serious. I have given this thought. Make no mistake what the gender issue does to those on other sides. Ogling is what men (strangers), do to women (strangers). All these events and controversies do confuse the issue. I do not want to be guilty of confusion here. There are few pleasures so warm and so human (human! I amaze even myself) but I offer myself to you uncensored) as that which we experience when we observe, in passing, a truly beautiful human person. (Human! I amaze even myself.) This is why, for example, the best paintings and photographs are either portraits or abstractions. The portrait captures the key foci of the pleasure; an abstraction explains the pleasure, i.e., why it is a pleasure. Last night after writing to you I went for my walk. I dared. I am brave. A young woman has stopped, and I see her, to determine where she is, or, perhaps, to rest. She is perfect. She wears black denim, black leather, and plaid things everywhere. She wears the denim as if skin. She is liquid and she is tense. Because she is tired and lost her eyes are wet and wide. Her forehead is high and proud. She has the pallor one only notices if the subject has naturally very dark skin. Which she has. Before I release my breath, before I avert my gaze, I think: there is no pleasure so warm, so human. Her nostrils have the flare of the impatient (or, my cynical self tells me, the flare worn by those countless young dolts longing to be exploited as pop-image copying the latest poses from TAXI and MODEL and CREAM). She is lost but not confused (or, my cynical self tells me, she is genetically at a loss for brain mass and matter—low on synapse).

The point is that although this is a pleasurable experience for me I would be ashamed if she found me looking at her. Notice, I did not want to harm, make love to, or abuse her. I don't even want to talk to the head holding up the mane of big wavy hair. I merely think of her: ah, here we have perfect. The night is all around her, cars speeding by, other people walking past her not noticing her catching her breath, deciding where she is, protecting her firm broad shoulders from the straps of her leather, denim and plaid packs and cases and purses.

So I am not ashamed but I would be if I found that she knew I was, well, ogling her. And ashamed that I am so cheap, so quick to assign beauty and grace, impatience and calm. She may not be beautiful, as we all know, this can only be determined in motion. She may possess a tight, tense, insipid little smile; she may have never performed a wide, laughing, all-inclusive smile; she may never have seen one. Her eyes may be bland, from staring at that perfect face gazing back at her too many times, practicing the flare of the nostril "Maybe I'll walk into a scout from the Ford agency" in the back of a synapse-free mind. She may have the most awful taste in music. She may not even care about music, listening to whatever is spun by the deejay, bouncing around in the predetermined bop. Fate is different for different people. Maybe I am just bitter that she, still young, has a forehead that goes on forever, and more than her fair share of hair.

Certainly not all of us have features such that we make up elaborate tableaux for passersby. It is not farfetched to imagine, however, that once, someone caught our profile off guard through a train window or over the edge of a row of cattle. But who cares? It shows, at least that the ogling thing is very complex. It's not an intentional crime. It's only wrong when it is planned by someone else for someone else. This is ridiculous, what I am writing here. Ridiculous. I know that.

There is a reason we do not put people on display and call them art-objects. We display their skills and call them artists or performing artists. Who could stand the shame of gazing at the subject of a photograph in reality? Just sitting there, posing with bruises and ropes and some animal or other panting. No. Ogling of that nature is best for photographs. And, yet, there was a reality behind that photograph. And, like other questions, theoretical or real, what needs to be discovered is what is the difference between gazing, warmth, beauty and ogling abuse reification. Was I wrong to admire the would-be model? Is it wrong to assign this title to her? I don't know her! She might be another god! She might be one of my letter writers! I don't know anything! Or anything about her! Would I be wrong to photograph people doing things they consented to doing and would do even if I weren't there? Would I be wrong to photograph them without their consent? Would I be wrong to force someone to catch the drool of a doberman after covering her body in bruises? Would I be wrong to look at this and not move? Would I be wrong to gaze at the photograph? To pay for it? Are these are not idle questions? I want to know the answers. I want to know why my hair is less and more me than my chairs are.

Well, you know I am lying to myself. Of course people "use" people in the flesh as art objects. I've been to sex shows myself; to vivant tableaux done gracelessly by junior highs—"I'm Desdamona and he's Iago." I've enjoyed these things. Well, you know, not really. This *is* ridiculous.

Oh and I know I know what is wrong for me. It is wrong for me to have used god. My problem: the minute I get any power I become as bad as them. I can't help it. I am into revenge. But do I have the right to hurt them for what some of them did to me? And, knowing the answer is no, why do I persist? Why did I waste my time revenging myself on *them* when god needed me? I mean it didn't turn out that way. I didn't use god. But I had *planned* to.

There is a relation between my concerns, my real ones, my theoretical ones, and why, when Hermione ceases to be a statue, we feel empty and wronged. What! Not a statue! Then the world and all that is isn't is nothing. Stopping the career of laughter with a sigh requires that she remain something, namely a statue. Otherwise, well otherwise, the pain is too real. It calls too much into question. Well, if my photograph goes in and out of human existence, then they can do anything and it's fair. Leontes is dismayed when Hermione comes to life. He feigns pleasure of course: it is expected of him. It is written into the script by the one who came any old way and in and out in and out from one sort of being to the next and knew that there were more than one kind of people too, always doing something for everyone. That one keeping every single one engaged. What! Leontes really thinks, the real Leontes what, not a statue! The elements inform against us all. I must share my grief with flesh and blood. And no wonder Thomas doubted. How much better if we all just stayed dead.

Photographs indeed. Roughly, I just want your affirmation. I want you to say, you the stranger who ogles me, who I force to ogle me, you wonder what does she look like, you curse that there is no photograph on the cover of this text, who is she, is she, is she more than one? Ogle away just don't let me hear about it. The solution is in the beauty of course. And I don't mean the perfect noses flaring like so many cobras. No. There is simplicity in beauty. Because there are only two kinds. Simple physical beauty: the beauty of a stone, a tree trunk long dead, glass on the beach which one takes to be a bit of bone, a human body which body we do not know. Conceptual beauty: the beauty of an object one has re-defined through knowledge. Conceptual beauty: the space between the toys I nail to my wall like so many martyrs, the rush of pain when it becomes clear that he's come in spite of your delicate dance to keep it alive a few seconds more, an infinite amount longer and the immediate realization that, yes, he can and will finish this task and with pleasure and gusto. Ah, the best beauty of all, the un-embarrassed lover. And, I find immense pleasure in imagining god move and talk; fingers that go on for ever and ever, lips that smile and move rapidly as eyes glance around, quickly, in the hope of catching a glimpse of all the ghosts in my house. Strangers with denim skin are simple beauty. But one takes one's pleasure where one can.

And after all visual beauty is the best next to the energy that comes from really good tactile pleasure, which, when honest, we all know is rare. Well, we have to make livings after all. And visual beauty is the easiest to destroy. Over exposure to visual stimuli does to the visual apparatus what too much noise does to the ears. So, I do not have a television. This saves my sight but turns me into a stranger to most people. Well it does. They don't know what I'm talking about. I don't speak their language. I know theirs of course because I read about T.V. which of course I can't help doing. Obviously.

Hah. I live in the paper and not the global village. Hah. You'd be surprised how many of us have made this switch. And remember this, and you should be frightened by it: PAPER WEIGHS MORE THAN SIGNALS. We, in the paper village, will win. We will smother you.

7. It is July 4. I am in the Land of the Free, the Home of the brave. Happy Fourth of July. I will go to see the fireworks after dropping one or two hits of acid. Traditions, after all, are traditions. That happy time, however, is hours away, thus I will continue this letter to you.

Here is a thought. There can be no thought which is not pre-thought or fore-thought. I didn't make that up. As you might imagine. Thinking now is to think out of time which is where we are not. Two attempts—three—to be outside of time. Nietzsche, Kierkegaard, Heidegger. All three ask: what matters most? This is what I ask: can I pretend to ask what matters most? And this is the difference between men and women because N, K and H, are, after all, first and foremost, men, they think they can ask what can be thought, they do it without dressing up for it, without masks, they make it the foundation of their thoughts. (And not, e.g., to what extent are my chairs an extension of my thoughts, of myself? Or, my hair?) No, I will pretend to ask "what matters most?" as if I am asking it really, as if this question already matters most to me. I pretend this structure. I find nothing. I have no answer.

Here come the deconstructionists. There is the text and there is nothing. The question? What matters most? The answer: I don't know but not the nothing. The answer could be finding the nothing through the use of discipline through Socrates, through the coming home of gods. The answer cannot be nothing itself.

Look God damn it. I'm sorry that you are bored. See we have a very strange country and we may as well admit it. I think these thoughts and express them to you and you are offended that these thoughts bore you. Well, look, I mean it is not as if someone has a gun at your head. Skip ahead. Have we lost our nerve to that extent. Skip ahead. Throw this away. Read a review. Tell someone you find it boring. Look. I really don't care. Here's a truth most people ignore or just don't know: unrequited love in any form is just idiotic. Do you even know what I mean? People spend so much time: Oh my mother doesn't like me. Oh my sister thinks I'm an ass. Oh he came and came in shuddering waves and I thought, my god, can I contain all this joy and pain? My god is it possible to have produced this depth of emotion? And like that and then the next day, it's like, well who the fuck are you? OK, everyone says well, it is normal to lose sleep over shit like this. I say, "There is only so much pain. There is only so much pain one can stand and then one gets a distance and says to oneself: "Self, it is idealist to suppose one's sister, one's mother, one's lover, whomever will continue to love you. It will not work out except sometimes. So, self, don't pine. Remember the day before. Remember that they loved you once in passing. Love them for the pain of not loving you."

Well, anyway, I'll cease boring you. That is my job, right? Once I adopted the demeanor of the great aunt. I expropriate the mask of restlessness and hysteria. Sitting and rising becomes a habit when alone. I sit back down. Lonely habits tend to spill into company after awhile. I sit back down. I was with god. Last June. What hard semesters we had both had, K-bone was hard.

I am with god. Last June. With the borrowed demeanor of the great aunt. That is, once upon a time I adopted the demeanor of the great aunt: I expropriate the mask of restlessness and hysteria. Sitting and rising becomes a habit when alone. I sit back down. Lonely habits tend to spill into company after awhile. I was with god—last June—and we had had hard semesters. I interpret this information telling, "Anne, you can't believe the hard semester I have had," as a conscious denial that I might have had a bad year, a bad life. I stand back up. It is summer. The trees which surround the window are sparse and dry. It is hot. I see the city—not just its lights. I watch the city. It is what I do this summer—last summer to you. I watch the city thinking: I have a life—a preparatory school job, an underground 'zine. I am not nothing. I meet with students. I read their papers and exams. I go to conferences. I listen to the latest in political theory. I am starting this new career of merely watching. I photocopy lyrics to thrash music and think about these young men entrusted to me. Then god catches me off guard. The breath that has been my life is whisked away from me. The game is destroyed. Watching will henceforth be an insufficient task. I may have to act consciously in a real world. In the meantime, while I reassess and revalue, I watch. I watch the game dissolve. I watch myself lose my breath over god who pants and moans. I watch.

When I was thirteen I lived with my parents. I studied. I socialized. I listened to music. One day I was alone in my parents' house. I sat by the window looking out at the trees, at the city buried by the trees. I was still. I contemplated: "I am doing nothing: I am watching the world outside the window. That I am doing nothing does not seem to force a break in time, does not seem to be a break in time: there is no respite from my breathing, from the awareness of time. There is no respite-like quality in this stillness. There is something to be aware of in this seeming absence of activity. But what?"

I notice the colors of the carpet, of the wall, of the window frames. I note the city buried by the trees. There is an immense joy in the noting. I am not nauseated by it. I have not noted that I am no longer alone. My mother has come home. She says, "Don't you have anything to do? Ever? If you have done your school work, which I seriously doubt, you can certain help me out who never has time to lay there growing idle hands."

Growing idle hands. I interpret her questioning, her commanding, as her conscious denial of my inner life. I stand up, making no allowance for her inner life, but how can I child that I am? I feel angry at her, guilty at being me. Well, and I still do. Why do I never have enough to do that I might say to some other "You could certainly help me out."

Until I gave up discipline I had been big on commitments. This is something I have done: make vows. That day my vow was never, never, never to deny another's inner life. And now, I watch for a career. I make other's inner lives into universes. I have no core.

It was years ago that I was thirteen with my mother. My vow now is that I not be interrupted in my watching—it is my essence to watch. I am interested in seeing. I believe in seeing but not in vision. Aesthetics but not art. I like fireworks but not symphonies. I like recordings of symphonies but not movies of fireworks. (They will put pop music to the fireworks tonight—in recent years they have done so in almost all North American cities—they will undoubtedly play Jim Morrison and the Doors performing "Light My Fire." I do not find this witty. It is not "enough" to rouse a smile. They will play "Born in the U.S.A.")

Have I told you that I have no television set? I rarely go to the movies although I do go to the movies. I do not need a camera to tell me what to watch. I make my own movies from my window. And they are better. I put music to tail lights and come in the rain. God says, "It is not consistent to reject movies and accept that awful music. Why that music then?"

Well. Can I help it if it is not known that music need not be visual. That it doesn't command me to do what it wants. I can use music for my watching. Movies turn us into slaves.

Books. Even books tire me recently. I have no patience for them. I say to god "Why should I read about the contradictions of capitalism? I can see them by looking out the window. Why should I read about emotions? I can understand them by watching the patterns of light going on in any city or town."

God never understands topics as these: the intensity with which they are avoided borders on rudeness. Showing that the point has been missed, words are mouthed: "You can see these things because you have already done the reading. You merely transfer text to your watching." I say "It may be a matter of emotional vocabulary. It cannot be a matter of reading. Whence the revolutionary moment in that case?"

As usual, I am right and god is wrong.

The demeanor of the great aunt is one of restlessness. I adopt it. I use it. It helps me to see things I had already seen through my watching but which I had not yet made plain to you yesterday nor to myself until now. Here is the thing: If one day you are walking down the street and you ogle someone you are invading her privacy. It is that simple. Leave your reification crap to others. You are where you ought not be. So, watching, as a career is not just simple. It has a code of ethics. It poses moral problems. It requires a great deal of thought.

The great aunt invaded one's privacy as a matter of course. I will never forget the morning after the night I had spent at her home when she came directly into the bathroom while I was putting on her best lotion. She was upset that I had not used the more appropriate for children variety kept under the sink for that purpose. I was upset that she had invaded me. Had noticed me doing what was none of her business. I will never forget trying to explain to my mother that no, I would never return to the great aunt. It seemed, and was, a small matter. But it is only small matters that distinguish us from each other.

The closer I get to the end the less I seem myself to myself. I find myself rearranging my priorities. I allow myself to think that my purpose in writing you is for your sake. I allow myself all sorts of self-deceptions. I lie to you, to myself. Who cares? Who could care less than I? I am afraid of god. I am afraid of you all. Discipline. Draw a picture of last summer or the summer before or that first summer with god. Draw the picture and be done with it.

I am going back to the first summer. A description, a drawing that shows the beauty of the mother. I am young. It is the last year of the worst decade of my life. (Not in my life but during the time I have been alive. The Seventies is surely the worst of the decades.)

And whose fault was that? Mine of course, I mean you entertain exactly one person in this, your only life: you. Do you really believe that when the people you call friends talk to you they are able to suspend their belief in themselves long enough to wonder about you? Why do you think you are always re-telling the same stories? Remember, then, it is not Anne's fault if you are bored. Presumably no one has a gun at your head saying "read for god's sake . . . your life depends on it."

When I teach and students look bored, as they, on occasion, do, I try to liven things up a bit. I tell jokes. I make allusions to pop songs. I move more quickly. I perform. I tell jokes. I play the clown.

Because I teach high school my students are essentially prisoners. I try to make their incarceration more pleasant. When I taught college I did not try to amuse my students. They were there by choice. They could amuse themselves as I amuse myself. One must know one's audience. This whole aside is unimportant in any case. It is absurd to engage in a dialogue the context of which presupposes that an aim in life is to be amused. The nothing itself, that which matters most according to some very knowledgeable persons, is boring. It bores us to death.

Discipline brings us back. The first summer. God, so long ago. It is very hot. I have nothing to do. I am bored. I had been drunk for a month. I do not use this term lightly. It is not an exaggeration to say that by many people's standards I am always drunk. I drink six or so glasses of whiskey a day. Two in the morning. Two in mid-afternoon, and, two at home with Xavier—with Xavier, now with whomever will do so, no more Xavier, finished, kaput. I am quite small. That summer I drank around the clock and I was doing nothing. I rarely ate. I seldom slept. I blacked out. I was bored. With no one to blame but you know who.

The phone rang far, far away. I can hear it ringing and think, "Dare I risk this being my mother who can always tell when I am drunk and who will not mention it but who will let her silence weigh heavily on me like thorns on dew drops?"

It is, of course, even the dullest among you know, god, calling me on the phone, I know, to get even with the others. The others who don't listen, who don't validate. Maybe this lovely-assed child will listen, will give validation. I don't mind. I understand this. I am used to it, the leering, the righteousness, the "one and only" discourse that rolls triflingly off tongues. I believed this once. It is sad not to believe it anymore it is such a nice sentiment. So it is somebody else's get even time. I don't mind. I am doing nothing in any case. I am intrigued. The actual meeting was in the winter: so sad that wine is not felt as it spills on legs. We are at a party and I am flirting with a women to my right and encouraged by her, forget that one of my hands is occupied and thus just sort of drop the glass and its contents on god. I go to apologize but *nothing* has been noticed! The morose, unfeeling stare, says, "Go ahead, enjoy yourselves. I see through your bourgeois pretensions. I, from my depth, lay the foundations for your shallow waters." Or something like that. I commit the women's name to memory. She has assured me she is in the book. I commit also to memory the roundness of her cheeks which far from giving the appearance of childishness roll instead into a long silky neck and a pointy chin the top of which is crowned, really crowned, jeweled, by the most beautiful mouth in history. Tight but full, red, red, red, but pale, a pink tongue so much a muscle, so little a sponge, teeth that look eager to bite, oh God a mouth to die for, I stare at it so much that she turns it into a little show just for me. Pursing the lips tight, tight, tight, showing just a touch of tongue, rubbing a tooth with lips closed. I all but pass out from desire.

Where was I? Where is my infamous focus? I commit the person to my right to memory. I turn to god, say something to which the reply is: "Can't you see that I am thinking?"

Incredibly, *I* apologize, thinking, God, well, think on.

So summer comes and everyone is bored and I am called in a

colossal game of getting even. Well, OK, I permit this. There is no blame in these games, right? Don't they just happen?

I can't find my discipline. Tomorrow I will tell you stories. I will tell you more of the story. Maybe I won't. For now I leave you to enjoy the Fourth as you see fit. I have already helped you with your Fourth. I will do my part for the ethos of my country. For better and for worse. I will attend the fireworks. I am and always have been enthralled (enthralled!) by holidays.

So now to the world, perchance to act!

BIBLIOGRAPHY

Acker, Kathy. 1988. *Empire of the Senseless*. New York: Grove Press.

———. 1990. *In Memoriam to Identity*. New York: Grove Weidenfeld.

———. 1987. *Kathy Goes to Haiti*. In *Literal Madness*. New York: Grove Weidenfeld.

Adorno, Theodor. 1979. *Negative Dialectics*. Translated by E. B. Ashton. New York: Seabury Press.

Agamben, Giorgio. 1993. *The Coming Community*. Translated by Michael Hardt. Minneapolis: University of Minnesota.

Aristotle. 1941. *Nichomachean Ethics*. In*Basic Works*. Edited by McKeon. New York: Random House.

Bachelard, Gaston. 1964. *The Poetics of Space*. Translated by Maria Jolas. Boston: Beacon Press.

Barris, Jeremy. 1990. *God and Plastic Surgery: Marx, Nietzsche, Freud and the Obvious*. New York: Autonomedia.

Bataille, Georges. 1988. *Inner Experience*. Translated by L.A. Boldt. Albany: SUNY Press.

Baudrillard, Jean. 1983. *In the Shadow of the Silent Majority*. Translated by Foss, Patton and Johnston. New York: Semiotexte.

Bey, Hakim. 1985. *T.A.Z. The Temporary Autonomous Zone, Ontological Anarchy, Poetic Terrorism*. New York: Autonomedia.

Blanchot, Maurice. 1990. *Michel Foucault as I Imagine Him*. In

Foucault / Blanchot. Translated by Mehlman and Massumi. New York: Zone., pp. 63–109.

Butler, Judith. 1990. *Gender Trouble: Feminism and the Subversion of Identity*. New York: Routledge.

———. 1987. *Subjects of Desire: Hegelian Reflections in Twentieth Century France* New York: Columbia University Press.

Cixous, Helene. 1991. *Coming to Writing and Other Essays*. Edited by Deborah Jenson. Translated by Cornell, Jenson, Liddle and Sellers. Cambridge: Harvard University Press.

———. 1993. *Three Steps on the Ladder of Writing*. Translated by Sarah Cornell and Susan Sellers. New York: Columbia University Press.

Climacus, Johannes. 1968. *Concluding Unscientific Postscript*. Translated by Swenson and Lowrie. Princeton: Princeton University Press.

Deleuze, Gilles. 1990. *Expressionism in Philosophy: Spinoza*. Translated by Martin Joughin. New York: Zone Books.

———. 1986. *Foucault*. Translated by Hand. Minneapolis: University of Minnesota Press.

———. 1983. *Nietzsche and Philosophy*. Translated by Tomlinson. New York: Columbia University Press.

———. 1988. *Spinoza: Practical Philosophy*. Translated by Hurley. San Francisco: City Lights.

Deleuze, Gilles and Felix Guattari. 1983. *Anti-Oedipus: Capitalism and Schizophrenia*. Translated by Hurley, Seem and Lane. Minneapolis: University of Minnesota Press.

———. 1994. *What is Philosophy*. Translated by Tomlinson and Burchell. New York: Columbia University Press.

Derrida, Jacques. 1986. "But Beyond.Open letter to Anne McClintock and Rob Nixon. Translated by Peggy Kamuf. In *Critical Inquiry*, 13, pp. 155–170.

———. 1988. *The Ear of the Other*. Lincoln: University of Nebraska Press.

———. 1987. "The Ends of Man." In *After Philosophy: End or*

Transformation? Edited by Baynes, Bohman and McCarthy. Cambridge: MIT Press.

———. 1988a. "Like the Sound of the Sea Deep Within the Shell: Paul de Man's War." Translated by Peggy Kamuf. In *Critical Inquiry*, 14, pp. 590–652.

———. 1982. *Margins*. Translated by Alan Bass. Chicago: University of Chicago Press.

———. 1974. *Of Grammatology*. Translated by Spivak. Baltimore: Johns Hopkins.

———. 1978. *Writing and Difference*. Translated by Alan Bass. Chicago: University of Chicago Press.

Erimita, Victor. 1959. *Either/Or*, volume I. Translated by Swenson and Swenson. Princeton: Princeton University Press.

Faulkner, William. 1929. *The Sound and the Fury*. New York: Vintage.

Foucault, Michel. 1989. *Foucault Live: Interviews, 1966–84*. Translated by Johnston. Edited by Lotringer. New York: Semiotext(e). Foreign Agent Series.

———. 1990a. *Maurice Blanchot: The Thought From Outside*. In *Foucault/Blanchot*. Translated by Mehlman and Massumi. New York: Zone., pp. 9–58.

———. 1990b. *Politics, Philosophy, Culture Interviews and Other Writings 1977–1984*. Edited by Kritzman. New York: Routledge.

Haufniensis, Vigilius. 1980. *The Concept of Anxiety*. Translated by Thomte and Anderson. Princeton: Princeton University Press.

Hegel, G.W.F. 1977. *Phenomenology of Spirit*. Translated by A.V. Miller. Oxford: Clarendon Press.

Heidegger, Martin. 1977. *Basic Writings*. Edited by David Krell. New York: Harper and Row.

———. 1962. *Being and Time*. Translated by Macquarrie and Robinson. New York: Harper and Row.

———. 1984. *Nietzsche: The Eternal Recurrence of the Same*, volume two of *Nietzsche*. Translated and edited by Krell. San Francisco: Harper & Row.

———. 1982. *Nietzsche: Nihilism*, volume four of *Nietzsche*. Translated by Capuzzi. Edited by Krell. San Francisco: Harper & Row.

Irigaray, Luce. 1992. *Elemental Passions*. Translated by Collie and Still. New York: Routledge.

———. 1993. *je, tu, nous*. Translated by Martin. New York: Routledge.

———. 1991. *Marine Lover of Friedreich Nietzsche*. Translated by Gill. New York: Columbia University Press.

———. 1985. *Speculum of the Other Woman*. Translated by Gill. Ithaca: Cornell University Press.

Kierkegaard, Soren. 1965. *The Concept of Irony*. Translated by Capel. Bloomington: Indiana University Press.

———. 1982. *The Corsair Affair and Articles Related to the Writings*. Translated by Hong and Hong. Princeton: Princeton University Press.

———. 1941. *For Self-Examination and Judge for Yourselves*. Translated by Lowrie. Princeton: Princeton University Press.

Kristeva, Julia. 1992. *The Samurai*. Translated by Barbara Bray. New York: Columbia University Press.

LeDoeff, Michele. 1989. *The Philosophical Imaginary*. Translated by Colin Gordon. Stanford: Stanford University Press.

Martin, Bill. 1992. *Matrix and Line: Derrida and the possiblities of postmodern social theory*. Albany: SUNY Press.

Megill, Allan. 1985. *Prophets of Extremity*. Berkeley: University of California Press.

Negri, Antonio. 1991. *The Savage Anomaly: The Power of Spinoza's Metaphysics and Politics*. Translated by Michael Hardt Minneapolis: University of Minnesota Press.

Nietzsche, Friedrich. 1980. *On the Advantage and Disadvantage of History for Life*. Translated by Peter Preuss. Indianapolis: Hackett.

———. 1969. *On the Genealogy of Morals and Ecce Homo*. Translated by Kaufmann and Hollingdale. New York: Vintage.

———. 1954. *Twilight of the Idols*. In*Portable Nietzsche*. Kingsport, TN: Penguin.

Putnam, Hilary. 1978. *Meaning and the Moral Sciences*. London: Routledge & Kegan Paul, Ltd.

Shannon, C.E. 1956. "A Universal Turing Machine with two internal states." In *Automata Studies*. Edited by Shannon and J. McCarthy. Princeton: Princeton University Press.

Siegle, Robert. 1989. *Suburban Ambush: Downtown Writing and the Fiction of Insurgency*. Baltimore and London: The John Hopkins University Press.

Silentio, Johannes. 1941. *Fear and Trembling*. Translated by Lowrie Princeton: Princeton University Press.

Smith, A.R. J. Assoc. 1971. Computing Machinery, 1: 339.

Spinoza. 1955. *The Ethics*. Translated by R.H.M. Elwes. New York: Dover.

Suleiman, Susan R. and Inge Crosman, eds. 1980. *The Reader in the Text*. Princeton: Princeton University Press.

Turing, A.M. 1936. "On Computable numbers, with an application to the Entscheidungsproblem." In *Proceedings of the London Mathematics Society*. C–42 1936, 230–265.

Wittgenstein, Ludwig. 1972. *On Certainty*. New York: Harper and Row.

———. 1961. *Tractatus Logico-Philosophicus*. Translated by Pears & McGuinness. London: Routledge & Kegan Paul.

Wittig, Monique. 1992. *The Straight Mind and Other Essays*. Boston: Beacon Press.

Wright, R. 1988. *Three Scientists and Their Gods* New York: Times Books.

Zizek, Slovoj. 1992. *Enjoy Your Symptom!* New York: Routledge.

———. 1989. *The Sublime Object of Ideology*. London: Verso.

DATE DUE

GAYLORD			PRINTED IN U.S.A.